GUN CONTROL

An Issue for the Nineties

David E. Newton

—Issues in Focus—

ENSLOW PUBLISHERS, INC.

Bloy St. and Ramsey Ave.
Box 777
Hillside, N.J. 07205
U.S.A.

P.O. Box 38
Aldershot
Hants GU12 6BP
U.K.

*For Jeff Williams,
my good friend and continuing inspiration.*

Copyright © 1992 by David E. Newton

All rights reserved.

No part of this book may be reprinted by any means
without the written permission of the publisher.

Library of Congress Cataloging-In-Publication Data

Newton, David E.
    Gun control: an issue for the nineties/David E. Newton.
      p. cm.—(Issues in focus)
    Includes bibliographical references and index.
    Summary: Presents pros and cons regarding gun control, discussing
such aspects as the history of gun ownership and access to guns in
America.
    ISBN 0-89490-296-2
    1. Gun control—United States—Juvenile literature. [1. Gun
control.] I. Title. II. Series: Issues in focus (Hillside, N.J.)
HV7436.N49 1992
363.3'3—dc20   91-23352
                                                                  CIP
                                                                     AC
Printed in the U.S.A.

10 9 8 7 6 5 4 3 2 1

Illustration Credits:
AP/Wide World Photos, pp. 9, 52, 59, 70, 100; Handgun Control, Inc., pp. 14, 65;
Library of Congress, pp. 20, 21, 23, 27; *The Miami Herald,* p. 36; National Rifle
Association of America, pp. 25, 31, 32.

Cover Photo: Comstock, Inc./Bob Pizaro

Contents

1	Gun Control: An Issue for the Nineties	5
2	Guns in American Culture	17
3	Guns and Violence: The Case for Gun Control	34
4	State and Local Gun Laws	50
5	Federal Gun Laws	61
6	Some Methods of Gun Control	77
7	Individual Rights: The Case Against Gun Control	85
8	The Future of Gun Control in the United States	98
	A Note on Sources	109
	Notes by Chapter	111
	Further Reading	121
	For Further Information	123
	Index	125
	About the Author	128

1

Gun Control: An Issue for the Nineties

It was the last day of classes at the University of Montreal. Staff members were assembling for a Christmas party. Some students were preparing for final exams. Fourteen of those students would never take exams. They were shot to death by a twenty-five-year-old unemployed man, Marc Lepine. The killer used a .223-caliber semiautomatic rifle on his victims, all of them women, and then on himself. Lepine apparently killed the women students because he hated all women, but especially "feminists." The incident was the worst mass shooting in Canadian history.

* * *

Kenneth Griffith, aged thirty, was upset with the police in Bettendorf, Iowa. He had called to report a burglary. But the police told him to call the county sheriff instead. Griffith loaded his .22 pistol and walked to the police station. Here he saw seventeen-year-old Sheryl Hovah sitting in a police car in front of the station waiting for a ride home. Sheryl was wearing her Explorer Scout uniform.

Apparently thinking Sheryl was a police officer, Griffith shot her dead. Then he turned the gun on himself and committed suicide.

* * *

Modessa Alvarez was wheeling her sixteen-month-old baby down a Queens, New York, street. Her three-year-old son was walking beside her. Without warning, a gun battle broke out around them. Nine men exchanged gunfire, apparently over some gang dispute. Suddenly, an eighteen-year-old boy involved in the fight grabbed Modessa's three-year-old son. He held the boy in front of him as a protective shield. A bullet passed through the child's left arm and into his chest cavity. The boy survived the gunshot wound.

* * *

Three San Francisco police officers responded to a silent alarm at a housing project. As they scouted the grounds, they saw a fifteen-year-old boy crouching near a building. The boy pulled out a handgun and aimed it at the officers. The officers fired their own weapons and killed the boy. Shortly thereafter, the officers discovered that the boy's gun was a toy pellet gun that looks very much like a .357 magnum. The boy, a mentally retarded child, was apparently playing "cops and robbers" with the police.

* * *

Sixty-nine-year-old Francis Boutcher of Boulder, Colorado, surprised a teenage burglar in his house. When the burglar tried to run away, Boutcher shot him to death in the back of the head. Boutcher was not arrested or charged for the incident. In Colorado, a person is allowed to use deadly force to protect himself and his home against "uninvited visitors." Some gun control opponents point to cases such as this one as a reason for private citizens having the right to own and use firearms.

Death by guns is a common occurrence in America. You can read stories like the ones above in the newspaper almost every day.

Sometimes the victims are famous people, like former President Ronald Reagan or former Beatle John Lennon. Far more often, the victim is an ordinary citizen like your brother, your aunt, or your next-door neighbor. One reality of gun-related violence is that it affects Americans of every kind, the rich and the poor, the famous and the ordinary, the young and the old.

In 1989, 18,954 Americans were murdered. Of that number, 11,832, or 62 percent were killed by guns.[1] On the average, one man, woman, or child is killed or wounded by a gun every 2.5 minutes in the United States.

People under the age of twenty-one are the most common victims of gun-related violence. Guns now account for 10 percent of all childhood deaths between the ages of one and nineteen.[2] In 1989, 1,897 children under the age of sixteen were killed by firearms.[3] Perhaps ten times that number were injured.[4] Of those killed by guns, about 1,500 were murders, about 1,300 were suicides, and about 450 were the result of gun accidents.[5]

Many Americans are horrified by these statistics. They look for ways to reduce deaths and injuries from guns. But people disagree about the best methods for solving this problem. Some people want to make it difficult or impossible for ordinary citizens to own guns. Other people want to punish criminals more severely. Still others want to expand and improve education about guns. Many other suggestions have been offered about ways to deal with gun deaths and injuries.

Honest, intelligent people of good will often differ widely on the question of gun use. So far, people with differing viewpoints have not been very successful at reaching agreements. Most discussions about gun use involve name-calling, hate campaigns, and political arm-twisting. It is easy to find pamphlets, articles, speeches, and legislation that argue for one approach to gun use or another. But it is difficult to find ideas, laws, and policies about gun use that most people can agree on.

This book reviews the current debate over gun control. It describes how the debate has developed through the years. It identifies the major issues involving gun use about which people disagree. It tells about the groups that have been organized to push for one or another position on gun control. And it outlines some possible solutions to the terrible costs of gun-related deaths and injuries.

Types of Guns

People often talk about "guns" or "firearms" as if everyone knew exactly what those terms mean. But they refer to a wide variety of weapons. Debates about gun use often focus on only one or another kind of gun.

One way to classify guns is by the way they are held. The term *handgun* is used for any weapon that can be held with one hand. Pistols and revolvers are two kinds of handguns. *Long guns* are weapons that you need two hands to hold. Rifles and shotguns are examples of long guns.

Guns can also be classified according to their caliber. When talking about guns, the term *caliber* refers to the inside diameter of the barrel of a gun, measured in inches. For example, a .32-caliber gun has a barrel whose inside diameter is $^{32}/_{100}$ inch. The caliber of a gun may also be an estimated measure. For example, a .38-caliber gun actually has an inside diameter of 0.357 inches.

Gun barrels can also be measured using the metric system, in millimeters. For example, a popular type of handgun is a 9-mm semiautomatic pistol.

Weapons can also be classified according to their intended use. Some guns were developed originally for use by the military. An AK-47 automatic rifle provides the firepower a soldier needs. Other guns are used primarily by civilians. For example, a shotgun is used most commonly for hunting.

Military-style weapons are sometimes referred to as *assault weapons*. Members of the mass media often use this term in talking about semiautomatic weapons. Groups advocating gun control laws often use the term in the same way.

Many gun owners object to this way of classifying firearms. They say that in the United States most weapons can be and are legally used by law-abiding citizens in many different ways. For example, some hunters *do* prefer using a semiautomatic rifle. Other gun owners use so-called assault weapons for target shooting. In contrast, weapons that would seem to have no military use—air guns, pistols, shotguns, and even muzzle-loaders—are still used by the military on ceremonial and other occasions.

Referring to a weapon as an "assault weapon" is not justified, they say, because of its negative connotation. Simply because these weapons have been used by criminals in a few dramatic mass murders does not mean that the vast majority of private, law-abiding citizens should be prevented from owning and using them.

Gun control advocates see the issue differently. They say that military-style semiautomatic weapons are far too powerful and too dangerous to be in the hands of private citizens. They argue these guns

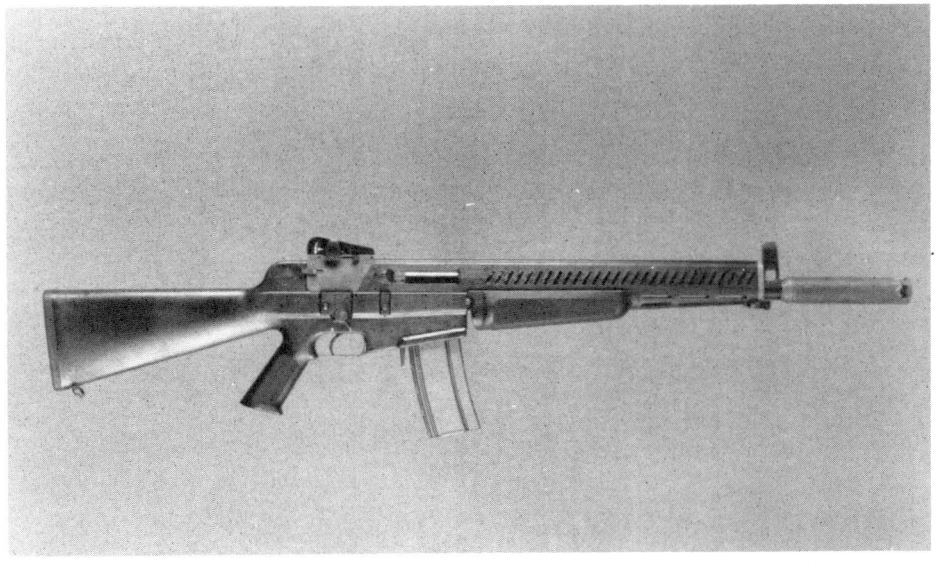

This prototype advanced combat rifle is an example of a long gun designed primarily for military use.

really are used too frequently as "assault weapons" in the commission of crimes.

This debate may sound like a dry, technical disagreement over terminology. But such is not the case. The argument centers on the question of whether *any* weapon is so powerful or so dangerous that its sale to ordinary citizens should be prohibited.

The Issues in Gun Control

The debate over gun use is very complicated. Many suggestions have been made for limiting the use of guns by civilians. And many arguments have been presented in favor of and against those suggestions. The basic issues, however, are somewhat simpler.

On one side, people who support some form of gun control say that guns are responsible for too many deaths and injuries in the United States. They propose that laws be passed that will make it more difficult—or impossible—for ordinary citizens to own guns.

On the other side are people who oppose all—or nearly all—forms of gun control. These people argue, first, that what we need to control are the people who use guns, not the guns themselves. Second, they say that gun ownership is a constitutional right in the United States.

One of the most crucial points that both sides of the argument disagree about is whether gun control works. Each side has statistics and studies to support its viewpoint that gun laws do or do not reduce gun-related deaths and injuries.

In fact, disagreements over the facts concerning gun use are common in this debate. Anti-control groups often disagree with the statistics produced by pro-control groups. Pro-control groups question the data published by anti-control groups. Even the statistical data published by supposedly neutral groups, such as the United States government, have been questioned by one side or the other. (For more on this point, see the "Notes on Sources" on page 109 of this book.)

Many people are somewhere in the middle of this debate. For example, some would like to find ways of reducing gun-related deaths and injuries without violating the rights of citizens to own guns. So far, those in the middle of the gun control debate have been too few and too weak to do much about resolving differences of opinion on this issue.

People with strong feelings on one side or the other of the gun control debate can join an organization that shares their viewpoint. Two of the best known gun control organizations are Handgun Control, Inc. (HCI), formerly the National Council to Control Handguns, and the Coalition to Stop Gun Violence (CSGV), formerly the National Coalition to Ban Handguns. By far the largest anti-control group is the National Rifle Association (NRA).

The National Rifle Association (NRA)

The NRA was organized in New York City in 1871. Its original purpose was to provide training in marksmanship for anyone who wanted to learn how to use a rifle. Eventually the organization broadened its interests. By the early 1900s, its membership included hunters, gun collectors, target shooters, ranchers, and others with an interest in guns.

The organization underwent a dramatic transformation in the 1960s. The violence of this period led to one of the nation's few national gun control laws, the Gun Control Act of 1968 (GCA). Gun owners nationwide became concerned about the growing threat to ownership of guns by private citizens. They became more active in fighting against gun control legislation. The organization through which they primarily channeled their efforts was the NRA.

Since the 1960s, the NRA has been at the forefront of efforts to preserve the rights of gun owners. In 1988, the organization had 2.8 million members and a budget of about $70 million. More than 350 staff members work in its Washington, D.C., offices.[6]

Legislators often acknowledge that the NRA is one of the most powerful national lobbies. It can, of course, draw on a large membership and a large budget. In addition, it is able to reach out to nearly 70 million nonmember gun owners and more than 13,000 affiliated gun clubs. When the occasion demands, the NRA can flood the Congress and state legislatures with letters and telegrams as efficiently as any lobby in the land.

The NRA works to influence gun legislation primarily through one of its departments, the Institute for Legislative Action (ILA). ILA has a two-fold purpose, lobbying and education. It makes NRA views known through four full-time lobbyists on Capitol Hill. In addition, it sends out more than a million brochures and articles each year on topics such as firearms ownership, safe firearms use, firearms for self-defense, and effective crime-fighting measures.

In 1976, the NRA established a second organization to influence gun legislation, the Political Victory Fund. The PVF is a separate legal organization whose purpose is to evaluate and support candidates for political office. The fund spent $4.5 million in 1986 and $3.9 in 1988 in direct campaign contributions, correspondence with members on gun control issues, and other campaign expenses. The NRA claims to have been successful in 84 percent of the 1,360 campaigns it became involved in during 1988.[7]

Both friends and foes of the NRA recognize its power. An opposing group, Handgun Control, Inc., claims, for example, that the NRA "has the money, the numbers, and the clout to influence and intimidate the Congress." The *Miami Herald* is even more outspoken in its views of the NRA, calling the organization "the meanest, most unforgiving lobby in the land."[8]

In addition to the NRA, other organizations that work against gun control include the Second Amendment Foundation, the Citizens Committee for the Right to Keep and Bear Arms, and Gun Owners of America.

Gun Control Organizations

Two of the major gun control organizations—Handgun Control, Inc. (HCI), and the National Coalition to Ban Handguns (renamed in 1990 the Coalition to Stop Gun Violence)—were formed in 1974. Although both work to promote gun control, they differ in a number of ways. For example, CSGV would like to see all handguns banned, with a few "reasonable exceptions." These exceptions include the military, police, security personnel, and sportsmen who lock and secure their handguns within the confines of a pistol club.

On the other hand, HCI supports a wide variety of legislation, including "a waiting period and background check for handgun purchasers; a ban on further production and sale of so-called 'Saturday Night Specials'; mandatory sentences for using a gun in a crime; mandatory handgun safety-training programs for handgun purchasers; and tighter requirements for handgun dealers and manufacturers." [9]

HCI and CSGV are also organized somewhat differently. CSGV is a coalition of thirty-four national social, religious, educational, and professional organizations. Among these organizations are the American Jewish Congress, American Psychiatric Association, Center for Social Action of the United Church of Christ, the Jesuit Conference Office of Social Ministries, and the United States Conference of Mayors. HCI, on the other hand, is primarily an individual membership organization.

Handgun Control, Inc., was founded by Dr. Mark Borinsky. As a student, Dr. Borinsky was the victim of an armed robbery. When he later decided to join a gun control organization in Washington, D.C., he found that none existed. So he formed his own organization, the National Council to Control Handguns (NCCH). In 1980, the NCCH changed its name to Handgun Control, Inc.

One of the early members of NCCH was N. T. "Pete" Shields, an executive at the Du Pont Company. Shields' son, Nick, was shot to death in San Francisco in 1974. Shields later became executive director and then chairman of NCCH and later, HCI.

Following Shields as chair of HCI was Sarah Brady. Mrs. Brady is the wife of former White House Press Secretary James Brady. Mr. Brady was shot and badly wounded during the attempted assassination of President Reagan in 1981.

Sarah Brady, chair of Handgun Control, Inc.

HCI brochures and publicity carry the slogan "one million strong." The organization's actual membership is probably smaller than that number, however. The NRA claims that HCI "may have 150,000 members" and that the one million figure includes "anyone who has ever contacted them." [10]

HCI claims responsibility for helping to pass bills banning plastic guns and "cop-killer" bullets, to prevent repeal of the Gun Control Act of 1968, to pass state gun control laws in California, Florida, Maryland, and Virginia, and to prevent the repeal of a "Saturday Night Special" law in Maryland in 1988.

In 1983, a third gun control group, called the Center to Prevent Handgun Violence (CPHV) was formed. CPHV is a nonprofit, tax-exempt organization that works to prevent handgun violence through education, legal action, and research. Some typical activities of CPHV include:

1. Forming a network of lawyers who will work for the rights of victims of handgun violence.

2. Sponsoring research to determine the nature and extent of handgun violence in the United States.

3. Developing and distributing booklets and pamphlets that describe the problems associated with handgun violence.

The combined membership and financial resources of HCI, CSGV, and CPHV are far less than those of the NRA and other gun organizations. The match-up between pro- and anti-control forces was demonstrated in the 1988 Congressional battle over a piece of gun control legislation, the so-called "Brady bill." In that campaign, gun control advocates spent $200,000 and the NRA $3 million.[11]

The gun control debate usually takes place between people in these two opposite and opposing groups who disagree strongly on the basic issues of gun use. In the remaining chapters of this book, we will try to outline what those issues are and how each group feels about them.

To provide some historical background, Chapter 2 reviews the role of guns in American society. According to various estimates, 60–70 million Americans now own about 140 million long guns and 60 million handguns. That is the equivalent of nearly one gun for every man, woman, and child in the nation.[12] Obviously, gun ownership is an important part of the American culture. Chapter 2 examines the way this love affair with weapons developed in American history.

Serious attempts to control gun ownership are fairly recent in the United States. The first federal law, for example, was not passed until the 1920s. In the last fifty years, however, the demand for expanded gun control legislation has increased. Chapter 3 outlines some reasons for the growing concern about gun use in the United States.

This concern has resulted in a handful of federal gun laws and thousands of state and local laws. Chapters 4 and 5 explain the purpose and effectiveness of these laws.

The term "gun control" refers to a wide variety of actions, ranging from complete bans on guns to simple registration of weapons. Chapter 6 tells about some of the ways in which gun ownership can be controlled.

Chapter 7 presents the position of anti-control groups. It explains why these groups are opposed to gun control and what alternative suggestions they have for reducing gun-related violence.

Finally, Chapter 8 looks to the future. It examines some gun-related issues that may be important in the next few decades and some possible ways of dealing with these issues.

2
Guns in American Culture

Mark's mother is looking for a birthday present for him. She wanders the aisles of the toy store looking for ideas. Many of her choices have something to do with guns.

* * *

Rosa is allowed to watch one hour of television on school nights. She looks through the evening schedule to see what appeals to her tonight. Among her choices are "Hunter"; "Columbo"; "Miami Vice"; "In the Heat of the Night"; "Midnight Caller"; "Jake and the Fatman"; "Guns of Paradise"; "Wiseguy"; "Cops"; and "Mancuso, FBI." If she picks any of these shows, she will probably see many examples of people using guns.

* * *

Pat is baby-sitting for three-year-old Donny Hauser. Before Mr. and Mrs. Hauser leave for their party, little Donny points his toy pistol at Pat. "Go ahead," Donny says to Pat. "Make my day." "Isn't he cute?" Mrs. Hauser asks. "We're training him to use guns properly."

* * *

Andrea is very excited. She has just been accepted at the NRA Whittington Adventure. The adventure is a twelve-day camp held in New Mexico. At the camp she will learn outdoor survival skills, big game hunting methods, and many other gun-related skills.

No doubt about it: Guns are a vital part of the everyday life of many Americans. According to one estimate, firearms can be found in nearly half of all households in the United States and a third of all Canadian homes.[1] What is there in our history that makes guns so much more important to Americans than they are to people nearly anywhere else in the world? Why are gun ownership rates so much higher in the United States than they are in European nations such as the Netherlands, Great Britain, and France and in other young nations of the world such as Australia and Canada?

Experts who have tried to answer this question see two factors of special significance in American history: the reaction of colonists to our European political heritage and the challenge of a wide-open new continent faced by our ancestors.

Guns and Freedom

Many pioneers came to the United States to escape repressive European governments. Those settlers were convinced that a powerful tool of authoritarian governments was gun control. They had seen that one of the first acts of repressive rulers was to deprive people of their guns. Without their own weapons, citizens were unable to resist the expanding powers of such rulers.

English pioneers had recent, firsthand knowledge of this fact. Between 1660 and 1689, both Charles II and James II had attempted to tighten their grip of power by disarming ordinary citizens. By the time James abandoned his throne in 1689, Englishmen had become "outraged and alarmed and finally convinced of the need to guarantee their right to own weapons."[2] Thus, with the ascension of William and Mary in 1689, Englishmen demanded a bill of rights that included a section declaring their absolute right to own guns.

Citizens of the young American nation remembered the role of firearms in protecting individual freedoms. The state and federal constitutions they wrote contained the same guarantee of gun ownership as did the English Bill of Rights. For example, the bill of rights in Pennsylvania's constitution stated that "the people have a right to bear arms for the defenses of themselves and the state."[3] Somewhat similar statements were to be found in the constitutions of the other colonies.

When the U.S. Bill of Rights was added to the Constitution in 1789, it contained an amendment, the second, that once again spoke about the right of private citizens, as members of a state militia, to own guns. The place of the Second Amendment in gun control debates is a critical one. Various interpretations of the amendment are discussed in more detail in Chapter 7.

Guns and Survival

Early pioneers had another, more immediate reason to own guns: to guarantee their survival. An important source of food for the pioneers were the wild animals they could kill. In addition, they needed guns to protect themselves against dangerous animals and to fight Native Americans. A 1624 survey in Jamestown, for example, found that there was an average of one gun for each colonist in the settlement.[4] At the nation's very beginning, the average American was convinced that "his personal safety lay with his gun."[5]

As the nation's population increased, people constantly moved westward to unexplored regions. Again, the gun was the pioneers' best friend in obtaining food, protecting against enemies, and conquering native inhabitants. Demand for guns on the western frontier gave rise to companies such as Colt, Lawrence, Remington, Robbins, and

Guns were important to those early Americans who ventured to the open frontier. This picture shows an early homesteader in the United States, with the weapons he chose to take with him.

Sharpe. Mention of these names still brings the image of firearms to many people's minds.

Formation of these gun companies led to improvements in gun technology. Weapons became more accurate and less expensive. Demand for new and better firearms grew throughout the nation.

Guns in Popular American Culture

Guns soon became part of the drama of the American West. Countless stories have come down through history about the partnership of pioneers, cowboys, ranchers, farmers, and their guns. The life of Buffalo Bill Cody provided one of our earliest folk legends. Cody showed how firearms could be used to conquer nature and tame the West. In one example, he was credited with killing 4,200 buffalo in a single eighteen-month period.[6] No wonder that guns were involved in the extinction or near extinction of many native animals!

A poster advertising the appearance of Colonel W.F. ("Buffalo Bill") Cody's wild west show.

Other characters from the western frontier like Wyatt Earp, Billy the Kid, Bat Masterson, and Wild Bill Hickok, have become American heroes. Some of these gunmen, like Frank Butler and Annie Oakley, carried the drama of guns in the West back to eastern states in "Wild West" shows. Tales of gunfights, like the one at the OK Corral, soon became part of American culture.

Although gun-related violence in the West was probably much exaggerated, Americans began to equate the excitement, freedom, and adventure of the frontier with guns.

That connection has become a prominent theme in modern American culture. A unique contribution of the American film industry, for example, has been the Wild West movie. Classics such as *High Noon, Bad Day at Black Rock, Blood on the Moon, Chisum, The Cowboys, Dodge City, Gunfight at the OK Corral, The Magnificent Seven, One-eyed Jacks, My Darling Clementine,* and *The Santa Fe Trail* have forever etched the role of the gun in American history. Some of the film industry's greatest stars—Tom Mix, Hoot Gibson, Gene Autry, Roy Rogers and Dale Evans, and John Wayne—earned their fame as gun-toting cowboys and cowgirls.

Some say the western frontier of the nineteenth century no longer exists. Strong, brave cowboys and their trusty six-shooters are rare. But Americans have adopted another group of gun-carriers as their heroes: the modern detective and policeman. In the late twentieth century, young Americans and Canadians have grown up with "Cagney and Lacey," "Crockett and Tubbs," "Kojak," and "Baretta" as their role models.

As a result, guns have become as American as apple pie. When people attack gun ownership, they are attacking a long-standing, very basic part of American culture.

Why Do People Own Guns Today?

The vast majority of Americans no longer use guns to kill the food they eat, to protect themselves from wild animals, to defend

An 1899 photograph of Annie Oakley, with some of the medals she won in gun competitions.

themselves against outlaws, or to attack Native Americans. Why, then, do nearly half of all Americans own guns?

The answer to that question depends partly on the kind of gun we are talking about. The table below shows the reason people gave in two polls that asked about gun ownership. Notice that the reasons given for owning guns have not changed very much in the years between the two polls. By far the most common reason for owning *all* guns is recreational. Nearly three-quarters of the people in both surveys said they owned guns for hunting, for target shooting, or for collecting. If you want to imagine a typical gun owner, then think of

Reasons for Owning Guns

Reasons	DMI Poll (1978)[1] All Guns	DMI Poll (1978)[1] Handguns Only	Time Poll (1990)[2] All Guns
Hunting	54%	9%	50%
Self-Defense at home	20%	40%	27%
Target Shooting	10%	17%	9%
Part of a Gun Collection	7%	14%	5%
Law Enforcement or Private Security	3%	8%	3%
Just Like to Have One	3%	6%	
Protection at Work	1%	5%	
Don't Know, No Answer, etc.	2%	1%	
Other			6%

[1] Decision/Making/Information (DMI), *Attitudes of the American Electorate Toward Gun Control, 1978* (Santa Ana, Calif.: DMI, 1979), as cited in Don B. Kates, Jr., ed, *Firearms and Violence: Issues of Public Policy* (San Francisco: Pacific Institute for Public Policy Research, 1984), p. 305.

[2] Jonathan Beaty, Michael Riley, and Richard Woodbury, "Under Fire," *Time*, January 29, 1990, pp. 16–21.

someone skeet shooting, someone hunting deer, or someone polishing a rare gun in his or her collection.

On the other hand, most people own *handguns* for quite a different reason. Notice that half the people surveyed in 1978 wanted handguns for self-defense and protection. Only a small fraction (9 percent) bought handguns for hunting.

These data are a little misleading. They report only the primary reason a person owns one or more guns. It is easy to imagine that a person who buys a pistol for self-defense might also use the gun for target practice. Or it is possible that a gun purchased for hunting could also be thought of or used for protection.

Hunting is one of the most popular forms of recreation in the United States, with 16,000,000 to 20,000,000 sportsmen licensed annually—many of them high school age and younger.

Patterns of Gun Ownership

What is the "typical" American gun owner like? In some ways, that is a foolish question to ask. Is it really possible to find *anything* "typical" about the 60–70 million gun owners in the United States? Perhaps not. Yet, it is possible to summarize a few trends among those who own guns.

Guns and Women. First, surveys nearly always show that men are far more likely than women to own guns. In the 1960s, for example, less than 10 percent of all handgun owners were women.[7] More recently, a 1989 University of North Carolina survey of guns and teenagers found that the rate of gun ownership among boys is twelve times as great as it is among girls.

But American society has changed dramatically since the 1960s. For example, in the last twenty years, the number of American households with no adult males has increased from fewer than 13 million to more than 20 million. In 1989, households headed by women accounted for more than one out of four American households.[8]

Some people think these statistics mean that gun ownership among women is likely to increase. Men have often argued in the past that they kept a gun in the house so that their wives could protect themselves when they were left alone. But what happens when there are no adult males in the household? Will women continue to depend on guns for their own self-defense and protection?

At least one gun manufacturer thinks so. In 1989 the Smith & Wesson Company began advertising its new "Lady Smith" .38-caliber revolver. The company claimed that its market research showed a potential market for the weapon of 15.6 million women. These women had expressed an interest in buying a gun within three years. Of this number, about 60 percent would be first-time buyers.

Smith & Wesson explained that they had designed the new gun especially with women's needs in mind. Women gun owners had previously complained that other handguns were too large and heavy for them. So the Lady Smith was made to meet "the physiological requirements of women."[9]

Following the same pattern, Charter Arms, a Connecticut gun manufacturer, is now selling a Bonnie and Clyde Pair for couples. The "Bonnie" is a .32-caliber magnum and the "Clyde" a .38-caliber special revolver.[10]

Some authorities see the changing status of women as a key issue in the future of gun control politics. In fact, two well-known experts on gun control, Franklin E. Zimring and Gordon Hawkins, have suggested that "the eventual solution to the American handgun stalemate may be found not in the *New York Times* but in *Ms* magazine and the *Ladies' Home Journal*."[11]

Regional Trends in Gun Ownership. A second trend among gun owners is related to place of residence. Gun ownership tends to be somewhat less common in the northeastern states than in the rest of

This turn-of-the-century woman illustrates the fact that women have often been handy with weapons.

the nation. In 1969, guns were to be found in about one-third of all households in the northeastern states. In comparison, 59 percent of all southern households, 51 percent of all midwestern households, and 49 percent of all western households contained at least one gun. These figures varied somewhat for various types of guns, as shown by the graph below.[12]

Gun ownership also differs among urban and rural households. As the graph on page 29 shows, the more rural an area, the more common rifle and shotgun ownership is. This figure probably reflects the use of long guns for hunting in rural areas. On the other hand, handgun ownership is about the same in all types of communities.

African Americans and Guns. The issue of guns in the African-American community is an especially difficult one. Many people—fairly or unfairly—relate violent crime with depressed, run-down, inner-city neighborhoods, often with a large African-American minority or majority. Drug use, teenage gangs, poverty, and gun violence often go together in people's minds. Many of us tend to think, therefore, that the misuse of guns is an especially

Gun Ownership by Region[1]

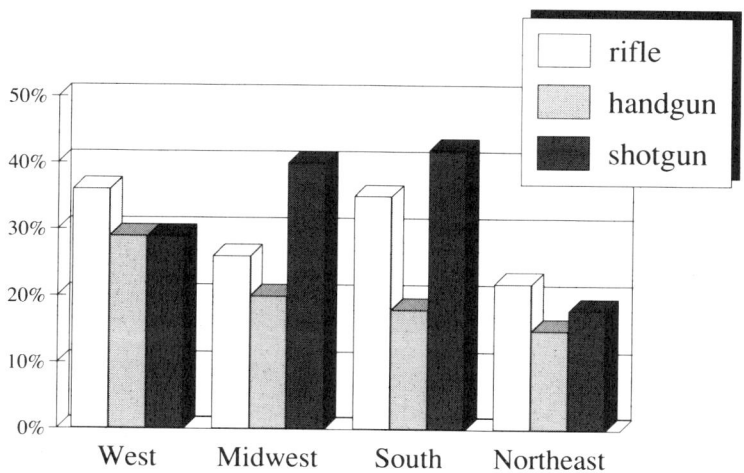

[1] Data from Newton, George D., Jr. and Franklin E. Zimring. *Firearms and Violence in American Life: A Staff Report Submitted to the National Commission on the Causes and Prevention of Violence.* Washington, D.C.: National Commission on the Causes and Prevention of Violence, 1969, p. 11.

Gun Ownership by Community Type[1]

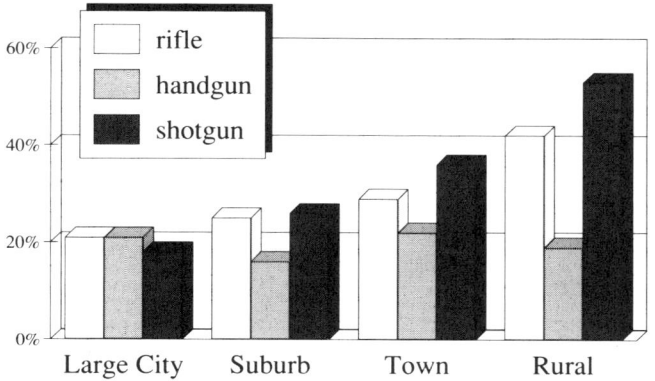

[1] Data from Newton, George D., Jr. and Franklin E. Zimring. *Firearms and Violence in American Life: A Staff Report Submitted to the National Commission on the Causes and Prevention of Violence.* Washington, D.C.: National Commission on the Causes and Prevention of Violence, 1969, p. 11.

severe problem in African-American communities. A recent survey on gun control seems to confirm that view. It concludes: "An astonishingly high proportion of black Americans have tasted violence firsthand in the lives of their families and close friends." [13]

Crime statistics reflect this problem. African Americans make up 12 percent of the U.S. population. Yet the involvement of African Americans in violent crime often occurs at a rate much higher than 12 percent. In 1987, for example, about 52 percent of all murders and 40 percent of all aggravated assaults in the United States were committed by African Americans. In addition, 45 percent of all murder victims were African American. Among those eighteen and under, African Americans accounted for 55 percent of all murders and 45 percent of all aggravated assaults.[14]

Yet surveys do not show that gun ownership is unusually high in the African-American community. A 1987 survey showed that 28 percent of all African-American households—in comparison with 43 percent of all white households—owned at least one gun.[15] And a 1990 *Time* magazine poll found that far fewer African Americans than might be expected owned guns. Of the 605 gun owners surveyed by *Time*, 6 percent were African American. Of course, it is not clear whether those surveyed in these polls were typical of the African-American—or the white—community in general. Members of gangs and of the drug culture, for example, would probably have been missed by either poll.

The interesting point is that gun control does not seem to be a matter of much concern to the African-American community. A review of articles in popular African-American magazines such as *Jet* and *Ebony* reveals almost nothing on the topic of gun control. Also, as Zimring and Hawkins have observed, both pro- and anti-handgun lobbies have "lily-white leadership." The reason, the authors suggest, may be that the African-American community has been "absorbed by other pressing problems." [16] The spread of the gun control debate to the African-American community could be one of the most significant events in the next decade, they predict.

Researchers have looked for other characteristics than these by which gun owners might differ from nongun owners. So far, they have not found any. In terms of personality, emotional stability, mental ability and other traits, those who do and do not use guns seem to be pretty much the same. As Zimring and Hawkins have said, "in view of the fact that about half of all households in America possess guns, this is hardly surprising." [17]

Guns and Kids

For many young people, guns are not some imaginary object they see on television or in the movies. They are real weapons that are part of their everyday lives from their earliest years.

In the first place, many children know that their parents own guns. They may commonly see the guns around the house. Responsible parents teach their children early on about the proper ways to use a weapon. They explain that guns are not toys but rather weapons that can cause injury and death. They store their weapons in a safe place where young children cannot get at them, such as in a locked cabinet.

But, in addition, many parents want their children to learn how to use guns when they are still young. One study by a University of North Carolina professor, Dr. Laura Sadowski, for example, found that nearly half of the 664 teenagers she talked with owned one or more guns. More than 20 percent of the gun owners had received their first gun by the age of ten. Most commonly, the young people in this study were given guns by parents or other relatives for hunting.

The National Rifle Association has long been active in promoting gun safety among young men and women. It publishes a special magazine, *Insights,* for its younger members. The magazine contains information on all kinds of weapons, notices of shooting contests, and tips on the safe use of weapons. Recent articles have included topics such as "Hunting From a Wheelchair," "Boys, Beagles, and Bunnies," "Ten Tips for Waterfowl Safety," and "The Soviet Shooter Development System."

Hunter education classes, which stress firearm safety and hunter responsibility, are usually offered by state game and fish departments. Most states now require that potential hunters pass such a course before a hunting license can be issued.

Gun companies recognize that young people in today's world are good prospects to become gun owners in the future. Many boys and girls today grow up learning how to zap aliens in video games. Gun manufacturers hope that this interest in video weapons will transfer to an interest in real guns later in life. Jeffrey L. Williams, president of Charter Arms, reflects this view. "Many people are exposed at a very early age to video games," he points out. "Once you go beyond that, a firearm is very similar in terms of hand-eye coordinating challenge." [18]

The availability of guns to young people troubles gun control groups. They say that guns are far too often the cause of death and injury among children and teenagers. The Center to Prevent Handgun Violence has provided the following statistics on this problem:

—Every day, ten American children under the age of eighteen are killed in handgun homicides, accidents, and suicides.

—Gunshot wounds to children under the age of seventeen have increased by 300 percent since 1986 in major urban areas.

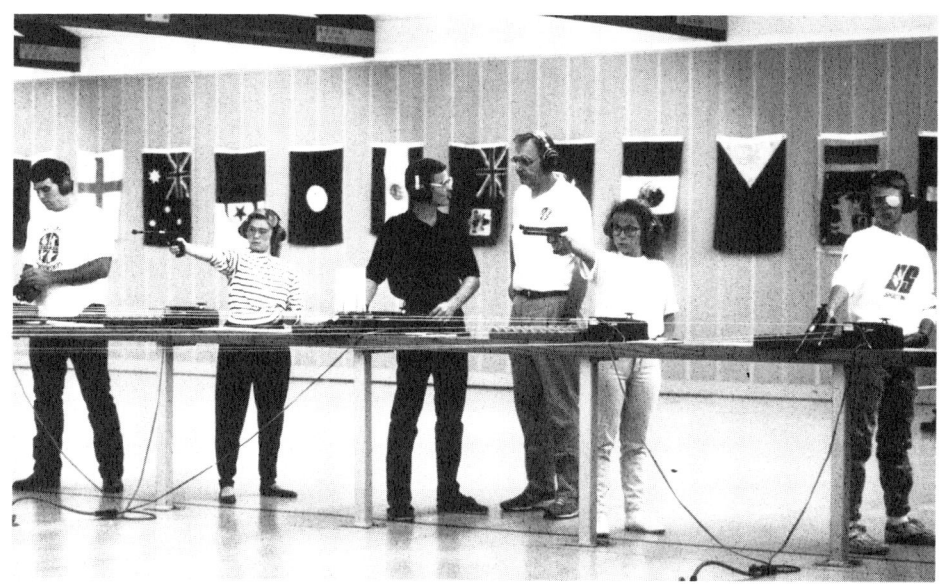

The NRA Junior Olympic Shooting Program gives young people up to age twenty the chance to compete at state and national levels in several shooting disciplines, including: smallbore rifle, pistol, air gun, running target, trap and skeet.

—In 1988, gun accidents were the fifth leading cause of accidental death for children under the age of fifteen.

—An estimated 135,000 boys carried handguns to school every day in 1987.

These facts are being brought home to families in many large cities. Students in New York City, for example, are taking to wearing bulletproof clothing to school. A company known as the Guardian Group International, of New York, reported in late 1990 that its children's line of bulletproof T-shirts, vests, jackets, and coats was selling very well, even at a minimum cost of $250 per item.[19]

The problem that some observers see is that guns have simply become a way of life for many children and teenagers. They are not unfamiliar objects they know nothing about but rather tools of everyday living. In a 1990 editorial, ABC anchorman Peter Jennings expressed the view that "a generation is growing up learning that guns are the way anger is expressed, disagreements settled, money is acquired."[20] When that happens, we can no longer be surprised when teenagers shoot each other in disputes over lunch money, basketball games, and girlfriends.

* * *

In conclusion, we can say that owning a gun is a normal part of life in the United States. It is a tradition that goes back to the founding of the nation. If you live in a typical community, about half the people you know live in households where guns are kept. On an average, those households have about three guns each.

People who own guns are, therefore, usually not very different from people who do not own guns. In fact, scientific studies of gun owners show that they are normal, average Americans.[21] If this is so, why has the campaign for gun control heated up so much in the last three decades?

3

Guns and Violence: The Case for Gun Control

"Year after year, thousands of innocent men, women, and children are slain by easily available handguns, needless sacrifices on the altar of congressional inaction and political expediency."

Coretta Scott King[1]

Guns cannot exist without death and injury. After all, the main reason that guns are made is to have a way of killing or injuring animals and people. Think of all the weapons produced for military purposes. The point of having those weapons is to be able to kill or wound one's enemies.

Even in peacetime, the point of owning guns is to do harm—or *to have the ability* to do harm—to other living things. Remember from the table on page 24 that three-quarters of the people who own guns in America want them for such reasons: for hunting or for self-defense.

Many people would probably agree that these are legitimate reasons for owning guns. And this would probably be a better world if guns were used *only* for these legitimate reasons. But that isn't the case. Too often, guns end up being used for purposes they were never intended for, for reasons of which no good citizen would approve.

For example, criminals use guns to carry out armed robberies. In 1989, about 180,000 robberies in the United States involved the use of some kind of firearm. In addition, firearms were used in about 190,000 cases of aggravated assault.[2]

Mentally and emotionally unstable people also misuse guns. The city of San Ysidro, California, was horrified in 1984, for example, when James Oliver Huberty went on a rampage in a local McDonald's restaurant. Huberty shot to death twenty-one people—men, women, and children.

In addition, innocent people are often killed or injured in gun accidents. You can read in a newspaper almost any day about young children who are killed or wounded while playing with a loaded gun.

These examples illustrate some of the reasons that people have for wanting stricter controls on gun ownership. Those reasons can be summarized as follows:

1. Guns are used by criminals in violent acts such as murder, rape, armed robbery, and aggravated assault.

2. Guns are used by ordinary citizens caught up in the heat of arguments, fights, and other kinds of domestic violence.

3. Guns are involved in accidental deaths and injuries.

4. Guns are used in most successful suicides (about 60 percent).

Guns and Criminal Activities

The point at which gun control advocates begin is that there is too much violent crime in the United States. They read reports daily about men, women, and children who are killed and injured by firearms. And they read crime statistics that show that thousands of Americans are murdered or wounded each year. They say these stories and these statistics tell us that guns are too readily available in the United States.

As this photo shows, children are sometimes the biggest supporters of gun control.

Almost anyone who wants a gun for some illegal activity can get one with little or no trouble.

While it is true that convicted criminals, mentally disturbed individuals, and certain other people cannot legally buy a gun in the United States, that is really no problem, gun control groups say. Those individuals simply steal the weapons they want, or they lie to gun dealers when they buy a weapon. The Bureau of Alcohol, Tobacco, and Firearms statistics indicate that at least 150,000 handguns alone are stolen every year. Authorities think that at least four times that number of thefts are never reported.[3] The huge number of guns in the United States provides, therefore, an endless stockpile from which criminals can get the weapons they use in their activities.

The most effective way to reduce violent crime, then, is to reduce the number of guns in circulation in the United States. This idea is at the very heart of most gun control activity. As one authority has said, "reducing the availability of guns would reduce all these deaths." [4] The idea is to make handguns more difficult (or impossible) to purchase. Then, criminals will find it much more difficult to get these guns, either by buying or stealing them. Without handguns, they will be much less likely to commit violent crimes.

Gun control advocates disagree as to how far to go with this philosophy. Some want to prohibit the sale of guns to nearly everyone except the police and other special groups. Others say that law-abiding citizens should have the right to own guns after they have undergone a thorough background check. Others say that only those with mental problems, young people, and criminals should be prevented from having guns.

Drugs, Gangs, and Crime

During the 1980s, the debate over gun control took on a new dimension. More and more often, gun violence was related to gang violence and drug disputes. Teenage gangs have been fighting over "turf" for decades. Previously, these disputes were settled with fists, knives, clubs, and pistols. Recently, powerful firearms have been brought into gang warfare more and more often. At the same time, gang members have continued to use handguns and sawed-off shotguns in their activities.

The city of Richmond, California, discovered this reality in January of 1990. During a one-week period, police recorded one death and seven injuries in eleven separate drive-by shootings. Authorities were unable to discover any specific cause for these shootings. Gangs of teenagers were apparently just angry with one another. As one Richmond police officer explained, "In years past, when teenagers had conflicts they settled them with fists. Now it seems more prevalent to go to the trunk of the car and pull out an Uzi or some kind of semi-automatic handgun to settle the problem." [5]

Richmond's neighbor to the south, Oakland, has become accustomed to gun-related violence. The city set a new homicide record in 1989 with a total of 148 murders. In the opening month of 1990, police recorded a rate nearly double that of 1989, with fifteen homicides. Nearly all involved firearms and drug dealings. For example, a twenty-four-year-old paroled cocaine and heroin dealer was shot to death at one of the city's busiest intersections in the middle of the day. The victim was apparently killed in a dispute over drug "turf."

In a second instance, a fourteen-year-old eighth grader was shot to death in an alley near his home. The police believed the murder also involved a drug deal. In yet a third case, a man named "Fat Dave" was killed by gunfire in front of his Oakland home. Police explained that the victim, a "drug enforcer," had previously survived many murder attempts including being shot and run over by a car and having a grenade thrown at his house.

Stories like these are not unique to northern California. They are repeated over and over again in every large city in the United States. They may well represent the most common violent aspect of the nation's gun problem today.

Some law enforcement officers now feel that those in the drug culture are often better armed today than are the police. In fact, this imbalance in weapons resources is partly responsible for a shift in police attitudes toward gun control. Authorities believe they need more help in keeping powerful guns out of the hands of criminals. They often plead for some kind of legislation that will give them a chance to fight back on more equal terms with those in the drug gangs.

Handguns

Nearly all gun control activity is aimed at handguns, not long guns. When people demand laws for the registration, licensing, or banning of "guns", they are really talking about handguns, not rifles and shotguns. The table below explains the special concern about handguns.

One fact that stands out in this table is the role of handguns in murders. Only about one-quarter of all guns in the United States are handguns. Yet, in 1989, handguns were used in 75 percent of all murders involving firearms. Handguns were used more than ten times as often as rifles and seven times as often as shotguns.

Homicides in 1989[1]

Type of Weapon	Total	% of Total	%of Total with Firearms
All Firearms	11,832	62%	100%
Handguns	9,013	48%	76%
Rifles	865	5%	7%
Shotguns	1,173	6%	10%
Other Guns	781	4%	7%
Total Homocides	18,954	100%	62%

[1] United States Department of Justice, Federal Bureau of Investigation, *Crime in the United States (Uniform Crime Reports)* (Washington, D.C.: Government Printing Office, 1989), p. 11.

Detailed statistics like those on page 39 are not available for other forms of violent crime. But experts believe that a similar pattern holds true for armed robbery, rape, and aggravated assault. They think that, when a firearm was used, handguns probably figure in half to three-quarters of such crimes.[6] FBI statistics indicate that, between 1979 and 1987, about 12,000 rapes, 200,000 robberies, and 400,000 aggravated assaults each year involved the use of a handgun.[7] The campaign to control "guns," therefore, is almost without exception a campaign to control *handguns*.

The Other Side of the Story

Those opposed to gun control agree with their opponents on one point: There is too much violent crime in the United States. But they say gun control people have come to the wrong conclusions in trying to solve this problem. Remember that gun control groups believe that an abundance of guns leads to (or causes) a high crime rate. Opponents of gun control say that just the opposite is true, that is, that a high crime rate leads to (or causes) an abundance of guns.

They argue that many factors contribute to an increase in crime in America. That increase troubles the average citizen. He or she feels the need to be protected against crime. So, the citizen goes out and buys the guns needed for self-defense. An increase in crime causes an increase in gun ownership, they say, not the other way around.

Anti-control people also refer to other statistics on gun ownership and crime. Between the years 1937 and 1963, they point out, gun ownership in the United States increased by 250 percent. In that same period, the number of homicides decreased by 35.7 percent. At a time when many more people were buying guns, at least one form of violent crime was actually becoming less of a problem. The pro-control argument about gun ownership causing crime was apparently not true during this time period, anti-control groups say.

Scholars have tried to devise research studies that would provide an unbiased answer to this question. They have tried to find statistics showing clearly what the relationship between gun ownership and violent crime really is. Unfortunately, those efforts have, so far, been unsuccessful. The studies that have been done have produced contradictory results. Each side of the argument can find some statistics to support its own position. And it can find reasons to disbelieve studies that do not agree with that position.

In fact, it is not even clear that "facts" are going to change the minds of a lot of people. People are often more impressed by individual events of special or dramatic interest than they are of statistical averages. For example, statistics show that travel by airplane is much safer than travel by private car. Yet many people read about spectacular airplane crashes and refuse to fly. They do not hesitate to ride in a car, however.

Similarly, people's ideas about gun control are more likely to be influenced by the image of President Reagan's being shot than they are by a book full of statistical tables. As Dr. James Fox, a criminologist at Northeastern University, has said, "People get their perceptions based on news, not on crime statistics." [8]

"Saturday Night Specials"

One type of weapon is of special concern to those who work for gun control. That gun is the "Saturday Night Special" (SNS) or "snubby." By one definition, these terms apply to guns whose barrel is no longer than 3 inches, whose caliber is .32 or less, and whose cost is no more than $50. (This is not, however, the only definition used for Saturday Night Specials.)

Some people argue that the Saturday Night Special has few if any legitimate uses. They say that its barrel is too short to make it very accurate, so it cannot be used for hunting. They also point out that the gun is made of cheap metals that wear out quickly, so it cannot be used for target practice. And they say that the SNS fires a low velocity bullet, making it a poor choice for a defensive weapon.

Anti-control groups point out that—in spite of these "flaws"—many citizens continue to buy Saturday Night Specials for their own protection. In any case, a Saturday Night Special has one important advantage: it can be hidden easily under a person's coat, in a purse, or in some other place on the person. That makes the weapon attractive to criminals who want to use a gun in a crime. For all these reasons, many people think that Saturday Night Specials are useful only to criminals. They point to certain studies of crime to support their views. In one such study, 30–40 percent of all guns taken from criminals in seven major cities in 1974 could be classified as Saturday Night Specials.[9] Banning Saturday Night Specials is, therefore, a high priority for most gun control advocates.

Those who oppose gun control in general are just as opposed to bans on Saturday Night Specials. They raise a number of objections to an SNS ban. First, they say, it is very difficult to specify *exactly* which guns are covered by the term "Saturday Night Special." Many small, light, inexpensive weapons used by people for self-defense might fall into this category. Also, many guns are small enough to be carried under a person's clothes. Does the size make those guns Saturday Night Specials?

Critics point out that crime statistics usually do not list separately the number of murders, armed robberies, aggravated assaults, and other violent crimes committed with Saturday Night Specials. The reason is that even criminal authorities cannot agree exactly on how to define this weapon.

Gun organizations raise some specific problems that banning Saturday Night Specials might create. For example, a number of gun experts recommend that campers and hikers consider carrying a *trail gun* for protection when they travel into the wilderness. A trail gun is a small, light, small-caliber, inexpensive weapon. The weapon could be very useful in protecting oneself against wild animals, these authorities say.

But banning a Saturday Night Special would probably make this kind of protection impossible. A trail gun is so much like a Saturday

Night Special that the trail gun would probably be banned by an SNS law.[10]

Finally, gun control opponents suggest an even simpler reason not to ban Saturday Night Specials. They say that criminals simply do not want to own or to use this type of gun in their activities.[11]

The Substitution Theory

Advocates of handgun control offer another argument for their position. They say, first, that strong control laws will make it more difficult for criminals to get their hands on handguns. That argument may or may not be true. So far, research has not provided enough proof to show that it is. But assume for the moment that the argument is valid.

Then, gun control advocates say, criminals will have two choices. First, they can choose to carry out crimes unarmed. Second, they can choose to substitute some other weapon for a handgun. Since knives are small, light, and easy to conceal, they would be a logical substitute for handguns. With either of these options, the number of violent crimes would probably decrease.

The basis for this "substitution theory" is that the weapons used in place for handguns—knives, for example—would be less dangerous than handguns. As the Coalition to Stop Gun Violence pamphlet on "20 Questions and Answers" argues, "It is not true that a handgun can always be replaced by another weapon; only handguns can kill with such certainty and chilling efficiency."[12] The pamphlet goes on to mention an FBI study that revealed that "firearm-inflicted wounds are seven times as likely to result in death to the victim as injuries by all other weapons combined."

Authorities point out that firearms work quickly and efficiently. When someone fires a gun, death is often nearly instantaneous. The act is over in a moment. The murderer has no time to think twice about his or her act.

An attack with a knife or blunt instrument is a different matter. A person may have to strike the victim many times in order to cause death. The person may have many minutes to change his or her mind about the act.[13]

Gun control critics point out a number of problems with the substitution theory argument. First, they say, convicted criminals are already prohibited from having handguns by the Gun Control Act of 1968 and most other gun control laws. Yet they seem to have no trouble getting these weapons. James D. Wright and Peter H. Rossi conducted a study of about 2,000 convicts serving time in prisons around the United States. Nearly nine out of ten agreed that "a criminal who wants a handgun is going to get one, no matter how much it costs."[14] Three-quarters of this number thought it would be "no trouble" (59 percent) or "only a little trouble" (16 percent) to get a handgun even though the law prohibited it.

Second, handguns may not be, compared to other weapons, as deadly as control advocates say. In one study of armed robberies, handguns were found to be only 1.31 times as deadly as knives. The conclusion of one reviewer is that "if knives were substituted for guns as a result of an effective gun control program . . . the savings in lives would be considerably less than would appear if the five-to-one deadliness ratio is believed."[15]

Third, criminals might choose to substitute a *more* lethal weapon rather than a less lethal one. For example, a sawed-off shotgun would be an acceptable substitute for a handgun in many crimes. In the Wright and Rossi study, more than 75 percent of the men convicted of crimes with handguns said they would be inclined to carry a sawed-off shotgun, 20 percent would carry a knife, and 8 percent would carry no weapon at all.[16]

Wright and Rossi think these answers should be taken seriously. They point out that 69 percent of the convicts they interviewed had already sawed off a rifle or a shotgun for use in a crime.[17]

Attorney and criminologist Don Kates relates an incident that illustrates this problem. He tells of a mentally disturbed man who tried to buy a handgun in a San Francisco gun store. The man was told that he had to wait several days because California required a "cooling-off" period before buying a handgun. The man, angry at having to wait, bought a rifle instead. The cooling-off period did not apply to rifle purchases. Immediately after leaving the store, the man, apparently angry about the incident, shot and killed four innocent bystanders.[18]

Domestic Violence

The amount of violent crime in the United States is one reason gun control advocates want to see stronger gun laws passed. A second is that about 60 percent of all murder victims knew the person who attacked them. That statement means that more than half of all gun violence takes place among acquaintances, friends, neighbors, and families.

Some people describe such crimes as "crimes of passion." They imagine a scene something like the following. A husband and wife get into an argument at the dinner table. The argument gets worse and worse. The husband loses his temper. In a moment of passion, he grabs his gun and shoots and kills his wife. She becomes one of the 22,000 victims of gun violence for that year.

Gun control advocates say that murder might not have occurred if the gun had not been available. The Coalition to Stop Gun Violence argues, for example, that "what might have been a black eye or a bloody nose often turns into a tragedy because of the accessibility and deadliness of a handgun."[19] One aim of gun control, therefore, is to reduce the number of "hot-headed" murders like this one.

The problem of domestic violence is one reason that some people want to ban nearly *all* handguns. Gun control advocates claim that such crimes are generally not committed by professional criminals, mentally or emotionally disturbed people, or other people who would be detected by a background check. Such acts are committed by ordinary citizens who just lose control of themselves for a few moments. No cooling-off period, gun licensing, or registration law would prevent these unplanned acts of violence. The only dependable way of reducing crimes of passion involving handguns is simply to make those guns unavailable to the general public.

Opponents of gun control say the statistics about crimes of passion are misleading. They point out that nearly three-quarters of all suspected murderers have long histories of violent criminal behavior. They say that people who are violent outside their homes are also violent within them. The NRA's pamphlet, " Ten Myths about 'Gun Control' " claims that crimes of passion murders occur in the vast majority of cases after months or even years of family violence. Truly "spontaneous" murders following arguments or drunken brawls, the pamphlet says, make up less than 10 percent of all criminal homicides.[20]

The NRA's position is that more severe law enforcement would reduce these supposed "crimes of passion." Police often know of families where violence is a way of life. The way to prevent a murder in that family is not to ban guns, the NRA says, but to solve the ongoing problem of violence in the family.

In fact, the NRA pamphlet sees a definite advantage in a family's owning a handgun. The presence of that handgun allows a woman to protect herself against a brutal husband. In Professor James Wright's view, " To deny a woman the right to own firearms is in some sense to guarantee in perpetuity to her husband the right to beat her at will."

Gun Accidents

Todd Glover received a .357 magnum police revolver from his father on his twenty-first birthday. Todd had long planned to follow his father in a career of law enforcement. He expected to use the new gun in his new career. Six days after his twenty-first birthday, Todd was killed by his new gun. The weapon apparently fired accidentally while Todd was examining it in his bedroom.[21]

* * *

Incidents like this one are, in some ways, the most troubling aspect of gun ownership. Each year, gun accidents kill about 1,500 Americans.[22] There are no good statistics on the number who are injured by firearms. But Wright, Rossi, and Daly estimate that in 1975 about 183,000 people were injured by all kinds of guns. The frequency of these accidents, gun control advocates say, is yet another reason to restrict gun ownership.

Surprisingly little research has been done on gun accidents. Probably the most famous study was done in Cleveland between 1967 and 1973. That study showed that a gun kept a person's home was six times more likely to cause an accident than to be used against a criminal. Gun control advocates often refer to this study. They say it shows how dangerous it is just to have a gun in the house.

Anti-control groups think the Cleveland study was poorly done. They point out that suicides were included with accidents in the study. In reality, they say, guns are much more likely to be used against criminals than they are to be involved in an accident.

Another study done in 1978 asked gun owners about accidents they had experienced or heard about. Four percent of those interviewed said they had been injured in a gun accident (2 percent) or had an accident without being injured (2 percent). In addition, 12 percent of those gun owners said they knew of someone else who had been killed in a gun accident, and 9 percent knew someone who had been injured. Finally, 4 percent knew someone who had an accident without injury or death. Overall, at least one in ten gun owners had personal knowledge of a gun accident.

The issue of gun accidents is complicated by the fact that most accidents involve long guns. Between 30 and 40 percent of all accidents occur during hunting. In addition, long guns account for 74 percent of all accidents that occur during cleaning and about 50 percent of all accidents resulting from playing and scuffling with guns. By one estimate, 90 percent of all gun accidents involve long guns and only 10 percent handguns.[23] If this statement is true, handgun bans may not reduce the number of accidental deaths and injuries very much.

Finally, anti-control people say that accidents are the price people have to pay for owning guns. Accidental deaths and injuries are, of course, terrible. Yet, gun owners argue, guns provide people with security. They probably save more lives than we can count. If some lives are lost by accident, that is unfortunate, but it may be a fair exchange for the advantages gun ownership brings.

Guns and Suicides

Each year as many as 300,000 people try to kill themselves.[24] In many cases, those people use a gun. About 10 percent of all suicide attempts are successful. Thus, about 30,000 people commit suicide each year. In 1987, 18,136 men, women, and children used a gun to kill themselves.[25]

The use of handguns in suicide attempts has been increasing at least since the 1960s. In 1960, 47 percent of the 19,041 suicides in the United States were committed with some kind of firearm. By 1977, 56 percent of the 28,681 people who committed suicide used a gun.[26]

The use of guns for suicides has become much more popular among women, children, and nonwhites in the last three decades. The table below compares the rate at which gun- and non-gun suicide rates have changed since 1960.

Increase in Suicides, 1960 to 1980[27]

	% with Firearms	% by Other Means
Women	116%	16%
Children	299%	175%
Nonwhites	160%	88%

Suicides are now the third most common cause of death among adolescents. In 60 percent of all teenage suicides, a gun was used. On an average, every three hours a teenager commits suicide with a handgun.[28]

These statistics trouble gun control groups. They point out that guns—especially handguns—are a simple, quick, and efficient way to commit suicide. "Handguns are unforgiving," they say. "They offer no second chance to consider suicide." [29]

Gun control opponents argue that a person who has decided to commit suicide will find a way to do so. If handguns are not available, the person will use poison, a knife, or some other means.

That argument is correct, control advocates say. However, many of those who attempt suicide really do not want to die. Their attempt is a cry for help. Using a less lethal method, they may have a chance to survive and get help. But a gun is "unforgiving." It may cause death, which a person really did not want to occur.

* * *

So people disagree about the way gun ownership and violence are connected. Some see guns as a cause of death and injury. They want stronger laws as a way of reducing crime and violence. Others see guns as an important means of self-defense and protection. The only laws they favor are stronger penalties against criminals. In the next two chapters, we will see what effect these two points of view have had on lawmaking in the United States.

4

State and Local Gun Laws

Some gun control advocates complain about the lack of gun laws in the United States. They may be right at the national level. The U.S. Congress has passed only a handful of laws dealing with firearms. But the complaint is not justified at lower governmental levels. By most estimates, there are well over 20,000 state and local laws dealing with guns.

The history of these laws goes back to the nation's earliest days. Even before the Revolution, for example, the Massachusetts Bay Colony prohibited citizens from carrying certain kinds of guns in public.[1]

Some of the earliest laws were aimed at keeping slaves from owning guns. White slave owners worried about what would happen if their slaves got their hands on guns. They feared the slaves would revolt. Thus, as early as 1640, Virginia passed a law prohibiting slaves from owning guns.[2]

Types of Gun Laws

Unraveling state and local laws on gun control would take a book many times the size of this one. It is possible, however, to make two generalizations about these laws. First, in the majority of cases, gun laws are aimed at handguns. Legislators are somewhat less inclined to place restrictions on long guns such as shotguns and rifles. This situation reflects the fact that most people think that violent crime is related to handgun, not long gun, use. However, many laws do try to control the sale, transport, and firing of all types of guns.

Second, most laws fall into one of two general categories, "place and manner" laws and "restricted ownership" laws. "Place and manner" laws allow people to own guns, but limit the way those guns can be carried and used. For example, many cities do not allow a person to shoot off a gun inside the city limits. Cities are crowded places, and the chance of someone's being shot accidentally is high.

Many "place and manner" laws prevent a person from carrying a concealed gun or from carrying a gun in a motor vehicle. These laws are designed to prevent criminals from carrying weapons with them. Of the fifty states, only New Mexico has no law concerning concealed weapons. Nearly half (twenty-one states) also require that a person have a license to carry a weapon in his or her vehicle.

The purpose of "restricted ownership" laws is to prevent certain kinds of people from having guns. People who fall into this category include convicted criminals, aliens, minors, fugitives from justice, mentally or emotionally disturbed persons, drug users, and alcoholics.

Enforcing "restricted ownership" laws can be difficult. The most common procedure is to have a person go through some kind of check before buying a gun. That gives police an opportunity to review the person's records. If the person falls into any of the "high risk" categories mentioned above, he or she is not allowed to buy a gun. Chapter 6 outlines some of the methods used to check out possible high risk gun owners.

This gun shop owner holds a stub-nosed .38 revolver. It is one of the most popular guns purchased in his store.

The problem with checking a person's records may be that the person *has* no record. Or they may lie about their background. In either case, the police have no way of knowing that the person is truly in one of the "high risk" categories. In that case, the person may still be allowed to purchase and own a gun.

State Laws

States differ widely in how seriously they deal with gun ownership. In general, states in the northeastern and midwestern parts of the United States have the strongest gun control laws. One of the nation's most severe gun laws is New York State's "Sullivan Law," which makes it very difficult for an ordinary citizen to get a gun. The law works on the assumption that a citizen should *not* have a gun. It is the citizen's responsibility to prove that he or she (1) really needs a gun and (2) is qualified to own and use one.

The law lists certain categories of people who may not have guns, and local police are permitted to add additional requirements of their own. A person may have to apply for as many as three different licenses: one to keep a gun at home; one to keep a gun at work; and one to carry a concealed weapon. Finally, police have the authority simply to state that enough gun permits have already been issued and that they will issue no more.[3]

The license application procedure can be very lengthy. The police may take many months to check on a person's background and to decide whether or not to issue the license. Even then, permission is very difficult to get. Keeping a gun at home for purposes of personal protection is usually not an acceptable reason for getting a permit.[4]

One writer describes the problems of a staff assistant to an important New York politician. The assistant had been threatened, so decided to apply for a gun license. The application was not acted upon. Even a letter from the Police Commissioner of New York City did not speed up the approval process. A personal telephone call from the commissioner finally got the process moving, and the license was approved.[5]

Massachusetts attempts to control guns in another way. There, the Bartley-Fox Amendment provides that anyone who carries a gun without a license or a long gun without a special identification card is subject to a one-year jail term without the possibility of parole or suspension.

Other states have no or relatively mild gun control laws. Western and southern states tend to have less severe gun laws than those in the rest of the country. As of 1987, for example, the following states had no laws restricting the purchase of a handgun (that is, requiring an application, waiting period, license, permit, or registration): Alaska, Arizona, Arkansas, Colorado, Delaware, Florida, Georgia, Idaho, Kentucky, Louisiana, Maine, Mississippi, Montana, Nebraska, Nevada, New Hampshire, New Mexico, Nevada, Ohio, Oklahoma, South Carolina, Texas, Utah, Vermont, West Virginia, and Wyoming. Most of these states did require a license for carrying a concealed weapon but had no other laws about carrying a weapon on one's person or in a vehicle.

In many of these states, local gun laws are stronger than state laws. For example, Dade County (Miami), Florida, requires dealers to have a license, to record all gun sales, and to report all sales to the police. In addition, gun purchasers must apply for a permit to buy a gun and must demonstrate knowledge of firearms and handgun safety.[6]

Some Trends in State Gun Laws

As the 1990s dawned, a few states began to take a stronger stand on gun control legislation. Episodes of mass murder involving the use of military-style semiautomatic weapons appear to have played a strong factor in some of these efforts. Mass murders in Stockton and San Jose in 1988 and 1989 motivated the California legislature to pass some of the strongest gun control legislation in the nation. Effective January 1, 1991, a fifteen-day waiting period was established for a purchase of all firearms in the state. As of the same date, all owners of semiautomatic weapons were required to register their guns with local police officials. (But also note the relative ineffectiveness of the latter law, as discussed on page 59).

In 1988, Maryland was the scene of another campaign to restrict gun ownership. In April of that year, the legislature passed a bill creating a new gun commission. The commission's job was to decide which kinds of guns could be listed as "Saturday Night Specials." Those guns were then to be banned in the state. The National Rifle Association fought against the new law. It organized a drive to put the legislature's action on the November ballot.

Many people felt the law would be overturned. The NRA had always been a powerful force in Maryland politics. But this time the NRA lost. The citizens of Maryland voted 58 percent to 42 percent to uphold the legislature's actions. The commission to ban SNS was authorized to begin work.

Local Laws

Local communities also take very different approaches to gun control. At one extreme, some cities, towns, and villages have voted to ban handgun ownership completely. Morton Grove, Illinois, took this action in 1981. Village authorities passed an ordinance making handguns unavailable to everyone but certain groups of individuals, such as police officers, military personnel, and licensed gun collectors. Since 1981, at least three other suburban communities near Morton Grove have followed suit. All prohibit the sale and possession of handguns by ordinary citizens.

The opposite view can be seen in the town of Kennesaw, Georgia. There the city council passed an ordinance in 1982 *requiring* every household to have a firearm. The council claimed that gun ownership would help reduce crime in the community. That plan seems to have had some success. In the year following adoption of the ordinance, violent crime in Kennesaw dropped by 74.4 percent. Burglaries fell from fifty-five to nineteen and rapes, armed robberies, and homicides to zero from three, four, and one, respectively.

The Morton Grove and Kennesaw laws really do not provide much information about the effectiveness of gun control legislation. First, crime was never a serious problem in either community. Second, in neither community was any serious effort made to enforce the gun laws.[7] Thus, it has been almost impossible to say what the effect of these local gun laws has been. In Chapter 5, we discuss in more detail the question of gun law effectiveness.

In recent years, the balance between state and local gun laws has begun to change. The National Rifle Association has taken the position that gun laws should be the same throughout a state. They have encouraged state legislatures to pass laws that prohibit local communities from passing their own gun laws. Such laws would not allow towns like Morton Grove or Kennesaw, for example, to have laws different from those of the state of Illinois or the state of Georgia.

One reason for the NRA campaign is that it is easier for the NRA—or any other group interested in gun control—to lobby state legislatures than local governments. Lobbyists would have to deal with only one group of legislators on the state level in Illinois, for example, not hundreds of groups of legislators at the local level in that state.

In 1988, the NRA convinced the Vermont legislature to become the thirty-fourth state to draft such a law. Thus, in these thirty-four states local communities can no longer adopt their own gun ordinances that differ from state laws.

The Problem of Semiautomatic Weapons

By the late 1980s, there was growing concern about a new kind of gun, the so-called "assault weapon." As mentioned in Chapter 1, gun groups such as the NRA object to the use of the term "assault weapon." They say that it has no generally accepted definition and carries with it negative connotations. In spite of this objection, the term is still widely used, generally with reference to automatic and/or semiautomatic weapons.

Automatic weapons are designed primarily for military use. They are generally small, light weapons that can be fired very rapidly. For example, the MAC-10, first used in the Vietnam War, fires thirty shots in three seconds with one pull of the trigger. Some other well-known automatic weapons are the Israeli Uzi, the U.S. Army's M-16 and its civilian counterpart, the AR-15, the H & K MP-5, and the AK-47.

Automatic weapons are also made in semiautomatic versions. A semiautomatic gun has most of the characteristics of the automatic version, but it fires only one shot with each pull of the trigger. The semiautomatic version of the MAC-10, the SM-10, for example, takes five seconds to fire thirty shots.

A semiautomatic weapon can be converted to its automatic form by using a commercially available upgrade kit and one additional illegal part. Private citizens in the United States can legally own a semiautomatic weapon, but not an automatic weapon.

By one estimate, Americans now own about 500,000 military-style semiautomatic weapons. Gun owners choose weapons such as these for a number of reasons. Some are gun collectors who want to own the latest high-tech weapons. Others use the guns for hunting. Still others enjoy Rambo-style target practice. Finally, as with any kind of gun, some people buy semiautomatic weapons to commit crimes.

The incident that brought concerns over semiautomatic weapons to a head occurred on January 17, 1989. On that date, an unemployed welder by the name of Patrick Edward Purdy opened fire on a schoolyard full of children in Stockton, California. He killed five students and wounded thirty more. Then he killed himself. His weapon of choice was a semiautomatic, Chinese-made version of the AK-47. Purdy had purchased the gun legally at a store in Portland, Oregon.

The incident brought cries of outrage from all sides of the gun debate. Everyone was horrified by the death and destruction involved. Gun control advocates pointed to the event as a terrible example of the carnage that can result from guns. They renewed their demands for tighter controls on all kinds of weapons, especially on semiautomatic ones.

Opponents of gun control said that the real lesson of Purdy's act was quite different. That lesson was that Purdy was a criminal who should have been in jail, not walking the streets a free man. He had already been arrested for the crimes of drug possession, solicitation for sex, illegal possession of dangerous weapons, receipt of stolen property, attempted robbery, criminal conspiracy, firing a pistol in a national forest, and resisting arrest.

The attack was neither the first nor the last mass murder using a semiautomatic weapon. But it raised an outcry among California citizens. Acting with unusual speed, the California legislature passed a ban on the manufacture, sale, or unlicensed possession of fifty-six military-style weapons. Similar legislation had already been adopted in a number of local communities around the nation, including Los Angeles, Cleveland, and Stockton itself.

On a national level, President Bush placed a ban on the importation of certain kinds of assault weapons. He decided not to take any action against the production, sale, or ownership of domestic models, however.

Anti-control groups are concerned about actions such as these. The NRA, for example, continues to oppose the imposition of a ban on any weapons of any kind. They point out how much alike certain "good" and "bad" weapons can be. They believe that it is impossible to ban only the wrong kinds of weapons. Any law that prohibits a semiautomatic assault rifle, they argue, could also be used against a semiautomatic hunting rifle.

Besides, pro-gun people often see *any* law as just the first step in a total ban on all guns. One gun owner, lawyer James Coombe, believes: "If you can ban an Uzi, you can ban a double-barreled skeet gun." [8] This argument is sometimes called the "slippery slope" position. Banning any one kind of gun, anti-control people say, is like standing at the top of a slippery hill. Passing one law is similar to taking one step on the slippery hill. After that first step, it's easy to slide all the way down the hill, to go on passing laws until *all* guns are banned.

Critics of laws banning assault weapons also question their effectiveness. For example, in the days after passage of such laws, sales of assault weapons often increase dramatically. People want to buy these guns before the ban on them actually takes effect. Even people who might not otherwise have wanted them may decide to get an assault weapon while they still can. Thus, the number of such guns in circulation may actually increase, at least for a while.

Also, banning one specific kind of gun may have little effect on the overall gun problem. In the year following Patrick Purdy's massacre of Stockton schoolchildren, the city of Stockton and the surrounding county of San Joaquin recorded forty-five murders, thirty-eight suicides, and five accidents with guns. Yet there was no

This Texas rally attracted many who oppose gun control. These people fear that a ban on semiautomatic and automatic weapons will lead to a ban on *all* guns.

public outcry to register, license, or ban any of the kinds of guns used in these deaths. How can people fight so strongly for control of semiautomatic weapons that killed five children on one day, critics ask, and then ignore eighty-eight other gun deaths in the following twelve months?

Battles over gun control go on all the time at state and local levels. In recent years, the same battle has been fought more and more often at the national level, too. Since the early 1980s, bills dealing with gun control have been introduced in every session of the Congress. Some of these bills are designed to make guns more difficult to buy and own. Others have the opposite objective. They are intended to relax the present restrictions on gun ownership. In the next chapter, we will review the history of gun control legislation at the federal level and trace recent developments in that area.

5
Federal Gun Laws

No huge book is needed to describe national gun control laws in the United States. Traditionally, gun control in this country has been considered to be a state and local problem. For example, the first federal law dealing with gun control was not passed until 1934.

Some people point to an earlier law, a firearms tax that was part of the War Revenue Act of 1919. But that was a minor piece of legislation that had almost nothing to do with controlling guns. In terms of gun control, the most important fact about the War Revenues Act was that it assigned the task of weapons regulation to the Department of the Treasury.

The Treasury division responsible for control of alcohol and tobacco was also given responsibility for enforcing the tax on weapons. In 1972, that division became known as the Bureau of Alcohol, Tobacco, and Firearms (BATF). Today, BATF is the federal agency that is primarily responsible for the enforcement of all federal laws dealing with guns.

Early Gun Control Legislation

The few instances of federal gun control legislation have followed widespread national concern about unusually terrible criminal activity. The first of these periods covered the era of Prohibition, from 1920 to 1933.

Most Americans are familiar with the outbreak of lawlessness that occurred during this period. Movies and television have replayed over and over again the stories of the way gangsters took over the rule of many U.S. cities. Mass murders with machine guns, sawed-off shotguns, tommy guns, and other weapons became far too common.

In response to this spread of crime, the United States Congress passed the National Firearms Act of 1934 and the Federal Firearms Act of 1938. The first of these acts limited the sale of machine guns, silencers, and other devices commonly used by gangsters. The second law went further. It banned the sale of guns across state lines by unlicensed dealers, and it prohibited the sale of guns to criminals.

For a number of reasons, neither of these laws was very successful. For one thing, the government never worked very hard to capture and prosecute offenders. Also, after Prohibition was annulled, Americans found other problems to worry about. The Great Depression that began in 1929 created terrible economic hardships for many people. Also, troubles in Europe and the approach of World War II took people's minds off gun control issues.

The next piece of gun legislation was not passed for three decades. Then, the Congress adopted the Gun Control Act of 1968 (GCA). Again, the motivation for this legislation was national unrest. The nation was seething with controversy over the Vietnam War. Protest, often marked by violence, broke out everywhere. The period reached its climax in the assassinations of President John F. Kennedy, Senator Robert Kennedy, and the Reverend Martin Luther King, Jr., and in the wounding of presidential candidate George Wallace.

The Gun Control Act of 1968 was largely a response to these acts of violence against national leaders. The act stands out as the single most powerful national statement of policy on gun control. It tries to deal with gun control from five angles. The first two are similar to provisions of the 1938 Federal Firearms Act. First, minors, criminals, mentally and emotionally unstable people, and other high risk individuals were prohibited from owning guns. Second, the sale of especially powerful weapons, such as submachine guns, was banned.

Third, the act prohibited the importation of Saturday Night Special types of guns. Congress believed that such guns were an important cause of violent crime. The problem was that Saturday Night Specials are also manufactured in the United States. In addition, some companies simply imported the parts from which SNS are made. Then they put the parts together here in the United States. As a result, the act was not very effective in reducing the number of SNS in the United States.

Fourth, the act prohibited the sale of guns across state lines. Gun control advocates had long argued that people who lived in states with tough laws could simply buy guns from a dealer in a state with weak laws. Finally, gun dealers were required to obtain a license and to keep very careful records of their sales. The idea was to make it easier to trace people who committed crimes using guns. If the gun used in a crime could be found, then dealer records would help the police find out who had originally bought the gun.

One problem with this part of the law was that many guns are stolen. Also, many are sold a number of times. In either case, tracing a gun back to a criminal can be very difficult. Also, dealers objected strongly to all the paperwork they were required to do by the act. They often claimed that they, not murderers and robbers, were being punished by the law.

Recent Legislative Efforts

Gun control bills now appear before the Congress every year. Some try to strengthen existing gun laws; others try to weaken those laws. An example of the former is the Kennedy-Rodino bill introduced in 1984. This bill was an effort by Senator Edward Kennedy of

Massachusetts and Representative Peter Rodino of New Jersey to strengthen the Gun Control Act of 1968. It was concerned primarily with Saturday Night Specials.

The Kennedy-Rodino bill would have prohibited the domestic manufacture of Saturday Night Specials and the importation of parts from which they are made. The bill received little support in Congress and died in committee.

In the same session of Congress, Senator James McClure of Idaho and Representative Harold Volkmer of Missouri introduced the Firearms Owners Protection Act. The aim of the McClure-Volkmer bill was to modify the Gun Control Act of 1968. Supporters of the McClure-Volkmer bill argued that the 1968 act had not worked. Innocent, law-abiding citizens were being harassed by provisions of the law, and criminals found it just as easy as ever to get guns.

The McClure-Volkmer bill eventually passed Congress, with some important amendments. The effect of the Firearms Owners Protection Act was to simplify record keeping requirements for gun dealers. It also ended the ban on the interstate sale of rifles and shotguns. Penalties for violation of some gun laws were also reduced.

Gun control advocates were able to save some parts of the 1968 act that had been threatened by the McClure-Volkmer bill. For example, one section of the bill preserved the ban on the interstate sale of handguns. Also, penalties were increased for the use of certain types of guns.

Both pro- and anti-control groups claimed that the McClure-Volkmer bill was a victory for their side. One spokesman for the National Rifle Association, for example, claimed that passage of the act was "a momentous day for American gun owners." [1] That response is understandable. Any reduction in gun control laws is seen as a victory by the NRA and its allies.

On the other hand, pro-control people were also somewhat pleased with the final version of the act. At least they were relieved that it had not done more damage to the 1968 act. Gun control advocates pointed out that the most important parts of the 1968 Gun Control Act had been saved.

A pamphlet from Handgun Control, Inc., for example, claimed that "in the final analysis, little harm was done to our nation's handgun law. In fact, the '68 law was strengthened."[2] For groups like Handgun Control, Inc., just hanging on to gun control laws, with perhaps some small progress, is a victory.

More Victories, More Defeats

The debate over gun control continues on the national level. In 1988, Congress considered legislation to impose a seven-day waiting period on all new gun purchases. The waiting period would allow police and/or the gun seller to check on a prospective buyer's criminal record.

The bill became known as the "Brady bill." It was named after former White House Press Secretary James Brady, who had been wounded in the assassination attempt on President Ronald Reagan in 1981. Thereafter, his wife, Sarah Brady, became a leader in the effort

Sarah Brady, of Handgun Control, Inc., at a June 5, 1990 press conference for the Brady bill. Seated at Ms. Brady's left is her husband, Jim Brady. A photograph of the attempted assassination of President Reagan is shown in the background.

to strengthen gun control laws in the United States. The bill was defeated in the House of Representatives by a forty-six vote margin. In a modest victory for gun control advocates, however, legislators did require the Attorney General to develop a plan for conducting "instantaneous" checks on prospective gun purchasers.

Two other gun control efforts have been more successful. The first dealt with plastic guns. These guns are made of materials that, critics claim, cannot be detected by screening devices like those found in airports. Supposedly, a person could carry a plastic gun in a briefcase onto an airline without its being detected. Security officials and legislators began to worry that plastic guns would become an ideal weapon for terrorists who wanted to hijack an airliner.

The NRA claimed that these fears were unfounded. In the first place, they said, the plastic gun about which people were concerned, the Glock 17, *could* be detected by airport screening devices. The September 1987 issue of the *American Rifleman* contained a photograph of an X-ray picture of Glock 17. Besides the NRA claimed, no plastic gun is commercially available yet.

In spite of these arguments, a bill banning plastic guns was passed by the Congress and signed into law by President Ronald Reagan in November of 1988.

Efforts to ban "cop-killer" bullets have also been successful. These armor-piercing bullets are powerful enough to penetrate the bulletproof vests worn by law enforcement officers. They are used primarily, according to gun control advocates, by criminals against the police. Many of the nation's law enforcement organizations worked with gun control groups for a ban on these bullets.

The National Rifle Association claims that it deserves credit for passing this legislation. As originally written, the NRA says, the bill was "so poorly crafted that it would have banned virtually all commercial available ammunition used in hunting, target-shooting, and self-protection." With the NRA's help, the organization points out, Congress produced a clearer, more specific bill that prohibits the sale of armor-piercing bullets to unauthorized buyers.[3]

The NRA implies that the bill probably was not even necessary. In the first place, the organization claimed, the bill simply wrote into law what was already "standard industry practice." In the second place, criminals had never purchased cop-killer bullets through normal commercial outlets. So passing a law against that practice would have no effect on a criminal's ability to get hold of the ammunition.

Action to change federal gun laws also continued in the courts. In December of 1990, the NRA filed suit in the U.S. Supreme Court, asking for an overturn of the 1986 ban on private ownership of fully automatic machine guns. The organization claimed that that ban placed the first outright prohibition on gun ownership by law-abiding citizens in the nation's history. It felt that the action violated its long-standing interpretation of the Second Amendment and that it must, therefore, be tested in the courts.

Gun control advocates were outraged. Prince George County's police chief, David B. Mitchell, said that, at the time the police were "taking [semiautomatic] Uzi's off the street . . . [they were] not equipped to face people armed with machine guns. They have no place in civilized society." [4]

The NRA explained why they thought this issue was so important. The Supreme Court has never ruled clearly and definitively on the meaning of the Second Amendment. If the Court should agree to hear and rule on this case, it would provide a crucial legal precedent on gun ownership that had never before existed in American law.

Do Gun Laws Work?

One of the major issues between pro- and anti-gun control groups is whether gun laws achieve the goals for which they were passed. Do they help reduce violent crime? Do they even reduce the number of guns owned within a city, state, or nation?

As usual, groups on both sides of the argument can find studies to support their own point of view. Or, in some cases, they can both look at the same study and reach opposite conclusions.

At first glance, it might seem fairly easy to see how effective gun control laws are. The first step would be to choose a city, state, or nation that had passed gun control laws. The next step would be to count changes that might have resulted from passage of the law.

For example, one could see if there were fewer guns in the city, state, or nation *after* the law had passed than there were before. Or, one could count the number of murders, armed robberies, or other violent crimes before and after the law was passed.

But studies like these are never simple. There are always many complicating factors that need to be taken into account. Consider the case of the District of Columbia's 1977 handgun law. Many authorities consider that law to be the most severe of any in the nation.[5] How effective has this law been in reducing gun ownership and violent crime in the nation's capital?

According to pro-control groups, the law has been very effective. In its pamphlet, "20 Questions and Answers," the Coalition to Stop Gun Violence claims that within three years of the law's passage, the murder rate in the district dropped by 25 percent. "Handgun Facts: Twelve Questions and Answers about Handgun Control," the pamphlet issued by Handgun Control, Inc., reports a 30 percent reduction in handgun deaths in the district during the same period.

On the other hand, the National Rifle Association's pamphlet "Ten Myths about 'Gun Control'" presents very different statistics. The NRA claims that violent crime rose by 43 percent between 1976 (the year before the law was adopted) and 1982. During that same period, the NRA claims, the number of murders rose by 14 percent.

The effectiveness of Washington's gun control law has also been studied by independent researchers. One finding from these studies is that Washington's crime statistics were probably not much different from those of other large cities in the late 1970s and early 1980s. One expert points out that in the years 1974–1975, violent crime reached an all-time high in many parts of the United States. True, crime fell in the District of Columbia after 1975. But then it fell nearly everywhere else in the nation.[6]

Of nineteen cities whose crime rates were compared to Washington, at least 70 percent showed the same kind of declines observed in Washington. Baltimore, the comparable city nearest to the district, experienced a 46 percent decline in murders at the same time that Washington was recording a 36 percent decline.

Considering all of these studies, one group of authors concludes:

> ... violent crime decreased in the District (and elsewhere in the nation) in the few years immediately after the passage of the [gun control] act ... but no persuasive evidence has yet been produced that this reduction was in any sense a result of the new legislative measure. [7]

New York City is yet another city about which gun control opponents debate. The residents of the city are covered, first of all, by the state's highly restrictive Sullivan Law. After 1985, they were also covered by a strong city gun law that required a mandatory one-year term for anyone caught with an illegal firearm. Gun control advocates expected these laws to reduce the number of guns in New York City and, hence, the amount of violent crime there.

Statistics have not supported that hope. The number of homicides dropped only slightly between 1979 and 1986, from 1,752 to 1,596. At the same time, the number of murders committed with handguns changed hardly at all, from 822 to 814. The number of felonies in which handguns were used also fell, from 33,519 in 1979 to 30,175 in 1986.

One problem with New York laws, gun control advocates say, is that too many guns are brought into New York City from out of state. What we really need, they say, is a stronger *federal* gun control law. One might have thought, then, that the Gun Control Act of 1968 would have helped with New York City's crime problems. That act made it more difficult to sell guns across state borders. Thus, the number of guns sold by mail to New York residents and the amount of violent crime might have been expected to decrease.

In fact, that hasn't happened. Violent crime in New York City is still on the increase. A late 1988 report on the city's crime situation pointed out that murder and manslaughter rose to near record levels in the first six months of that year. Violent crimes in every other area were also up. As Thomas Repetto, head of the Citizens Crime Commission, said, "These numbers are very, very bad." [8]

Another problem in New York City seems to be that the mandatory one-year sentence is not enforced very often. Someone convicted of carrying a gun illegally has only a one in three chance of actually being sentenced. Half of those convicted under the law so far have served no jail time at all. Although the law may have seemed like a good idea when it was passed, it has not achieved the objectives that gun control advocates had hoped for. Part of the problem seems to be that enforcement has been inadequate. Also, some observers feel that the law contained too many loopholes to be really effective.[9]

New York Police Commissioner Lee Brown displays some of the 16,000 guns confiscated by police in 1989. Like many other American cities, New York City has difficulty controlling its high crime rate.

Examples like the District of Columbia and New York City situations can be repeated over and over again. For every example of effective gun control, anti-control groups can find any number of errors, misunderstandings, and misinterpretations.

Another example is the research done on the effectiveness of the Bartley-Fox amendment in Massachusetts, which was passed by the Massachusetts legislature in 1974. It imposed a mandatory one-year sentence for any person carrying a gun without a proper permit. Did the amendment help reduce violent crime in Massachusetts?

Again, gun control advocates say that it did. Handgun Control, Inc., for example, claims that the new law caused a drop of nearly 50 percent in handgun murders and a decline of 35 percent in armed robberies in Boston.[10]

But you get different results by looking at short-term changes compared to long-term changes, anti-control groups say. In fact, they argue that ten years after the law was passed the murder rate in Boston is right back where it would have been without the law. Gun control advocates agree that murder rates may have returned to their original rates in Boston, but they say that the number of homicides and assaults *committed with a gun* has not.

In addition, critics say, the situation in other parts of Massachusetts was very different from what it was in Boston. Crime rates in other Massachusetts cities never dropped after the law was put into effect. And, as in the District of Columbia case, trends in Boston at the time were not very different from those in neighboring cities and states.

Finally, the NRA argues, the Bartley-Fox amendment was not even a *gun control* law. Nothing in the law attempted to restrict the purchase of guns, as most control laws do. Instead, the law called for stronger punishment of people found carrying a gun, usually in the commission of a crime.

That kind of stronger enforcement legislation is just what anti-control groups have been demanding, said the NRA. Even given these good intentions, however, the NRA claims that the Bartley-Fox amendment was rarely employed against criminals who used firearms in the commission of a crime.[11]

A highly controversial study on gun law effectiveness was reported in May 1989. A team of researchers from the Universities of Washington, British Columbia, and Tennessee, led by John H. Sloan, reported on a study on gun-related violence in two nearby cities, Seattle, Washington, and Vancouver, British Columbia. They selected these two cities because they were alike in many ways: geographically, culturally, and demographically. One way in which they differed is that Vancouver has very strict gun control laws, while Seattle has very lenient gun laws.

The Sloan team reported that during a two-year period from 1987 through 1988, Seattle recorded 139 homicides involving handguns out of a total of 388, a 36 percent rate of deaths by handguns. In Vancouver, handguns were responsible for twenty-five deaths out of 204 homicides, a rate of 12 percent. The researchers concluded that a Seattle resident was 1.6 times more likely to be murdered than a resident of Vancouver. That difference, they said, reflected the greater ease of owning a handgun in Seattle.[12]

Opponents of gun control responded quickly and angrily to the study. They claimed that Seattle and Vancouver were much more different than Dr. Sloan's team had claimed. The strongest criticisms came from Dr. Paul H. Blackman, director of research for the National Rifle Association. Dr. Blackman claimed: "There is nothing in the [Sloan] paper that could possibly be mistaken for scientific methods by a sociologist or criminologist." [13]

International Comparisons

Another aspect of this argument appears in almost every pamphlet on gun control: how gun laws and violent crime in the United States compare with those in other countries around the world.

The way countries deal with gun ownership varies widely. In Switzerland, for example, every man is a member of the national militia. He is required to keep a long gun and ammunition in his home. Yet the murder rate in Switzerland is about 15 percent of that in the United States. Anti-control groups say these facts prove that simply having guns in the house does not lead to their use in violent crime.[14]

Gun Control advocates say that this argument misses the point. People most often use handguns, not long guns, to commit violent crimes. And handguns are carefully regulated in Switzerland. A person must have a background check, must get a permit for the gun, and must register with the government. Access to the most dangerous weapons—handguns—is therefore carefully controlled in Switzerland.

Two other nations that opponents argue about are England and Japan. (Indeed, one author has suggested, "In the world of gun control, there seem to be only three foreign countries: Great Britain, Japan, and Switzerland."[15]) Japan has highly restrictive gun laws. In fact, private ownership of guns is prohibited in Japan. As a result, gun control advocates say, violent crime is nearly nonexistent in that nation. In 1983, for example, only thirty-five people were murdered by handguns in all of Japan compared to 9,014 in the United States. Although our population is only twice as large as Japan's, our handgun murder rate is 250 times as great.[16]

Gun control opponents say that gun laws are not the reason for Japan's low crime rate. The Japanese simply have a different cultural tradition from that of the United States. They have a greater respect for law and order than do Americans. Lower murder rates in Japan are a cultural effect, they say, not the result of gun laws. As evidence of this fact, opponents point out that the murder rate among Japanese Americans, who have the same access to guns as other Americans, is even lower than it is among the Japanese.[17]

For many years, gun control advocates used England as its prime example of effective gun control laws. They have pointed out that the rate of violent crime in England is very low. Even police officers normally do not carry weapons. In 1983, for example, there were only eight handgun murders in all of England, even fewer than in Japan.[18]

Anti-control groups cannot argue about cultural differences in this case, say control advocates. The United States and England certainly share a common cultural tradition. So stronger gun laws in England must account for the low rate of violent crime there, they say.

The NRA disagrees. British and U.S. legal traditions are actually quite different, they say. As an example, English law enforcement officers can search without a warrant and can deny counsel to suspected criminals. Neither action is permitted under U.S. law.

Furthermore, the NRA points to rising crime rates in England during the last decade. The number of armed robberies involving handguns in England rose by 700 percent between 1974 and 1986, they say.[19] During that same period, the number of armed robberies in the United States fell by 17 percent.

Besides, the NRA suggests, if one really wants to make comparisons, they should be between the United States and Northern Ireland, not England. Northern Ireland has even stronger handgun laws than does England. Yet, one can hardly argue that these laws have kept Northern Ireland free from handgun-related violence.[20]

What Do the People Want?

Most good laws reflect the will of the majority of the people. So each side of the gun control debate tries to show that most Americans agree with its point of view. For example, Handgun Control, Inc., cites a 1981 Gallup poll that found that "91% of Americans support a waiting period and background check for handgun purchases."[21]

In 1990 *Time* magazine commissioned a poll of gun owners in the United States. The poll showed that 87 percent of the gun owners asked favored a federal law requiring a seven-day waiting period and background check for anyone wanting to buy a handgun. At least half also favored mandatory registration of rifles (54 percent of those asked), shotguns (50 percent), handguns (72 percent), and semiautomatic weapons (73 percent.)[22]

Results like these occur over and over again in public opinion polls. When people are asked specifically if they favor some form of gun control, they tend to say "yes." A review of two large national surveys showed that "large majorities favor any measure involving the registration or licensing of *handguns,* both for new purchases and for handguns presently owned." [23]

Polls do show that a majority of people believe they have a right to own guns. Yet even a majority of those who hold this view believe that some form of control on gun ownership is necessary.

Those opposed to gun control interpret these results in a different way. They say that questions in most polls are biased. The questions tend to make people answer in a particular way, usually in favor of gun control. By way of comparison, gun control opponents point to quite different results obtained in two polls commissioned by the National Rifle Association in 1975 and 1978.

In these polls, respondents were not specifically asked if they favored one kind of gun control or another. Instead, they were asked what they thought should be done about rising crime rates. In this case, only about 10 percent of the respondents volunteered any answer related to the idea of gun control. The researchers concluded that "gun control . . . does not spontaneously occur to voters as an anti-crime measure." [24]

Instead, the vast majority of those interviewed for the poll (93 percent) favored strict mandatory penalties for criminals who use firearms in a crime. Of course, this position is also that of the NRA, who paid for the poll.

Opponents of gun control argue that the best test of public opinion on gun control is an election. What people tell a pollster and how they vote on a gun control law can be very different, they say. In two earlier state elections, citizens have had the chance to say exactly how they feel about some aspect of gun control.

In November 1976, a Massachusetts referendum called for a ban on all handguns. That proposal was defeated by a margin of more than two to one. Six years later, California voters were asked to vote on an initiative that would have required all handguns to be registered. The initiative would also have limited the number of handguns allowed in the state. That initiative also failed, by a margin of 63 percent to 37 percent.

The 1988 Maryland referendum on the state's handgun law produced different results. In that case, the state upheld the legislature's decision to ban certain types of guns. There is no way of knowing if the Maryland results represent a new trend in the nation or if they are a single, isolated episode in gun control voting.

* * *

Each side in the gun control debate believes that it represents the will of the majority of the people. And, in some respects, each side is correct. People in the middle of this debate hope that some day the two sides will find points on which they can agree. If and when that agreement comes, it may take the form of one of the proposals described in the next chapter.

6

Some Methods of Gun Control

As mayor of Pleasant City, you are worried about violent crime in your town. You wonder what action you can take to deal with this problem. What are your choices?

Governmental officials and private citizens throughout the United States have thought about that question for years. They have come up with about six major ideas. They are:

1. More severe penalties for convicted criminals.

2. Licensing of gun dealers.

3. Registration of guns.

4. Permissive licensing of gun owners.

5. Restrictive licensing of gun owners.

6. Bans on guns (almost always, handguns).

More Severe Penalties

"America does not have a gun problem. We have a criminal problem." [1]

Traditionally, the National Rifle Association and other anti-control groups have favored only one of these options: more severe penalties for people convicted of gun-related crimes. These groups say that governments, police, and the courts are too easy on criminals. Far too often, a person who uses a gun in a crime is not caught. If the criminal is caught, he or she is set free too quickly. That same person just goes out and commits another gun-related crime, these groups argue. The way to stop violent crime, they say, is not to ban guns, but to prosecute the criminals who use them.

This position is summed up in one of the NRA's best known slogans: "Guns don't kill people; people kill people." That slogan means that laws should be aimed at those who use guns, not at the guns themselves. The NRA's position on gun control is that the nation must: "reform and strengthen our federal and state criminal justice systems. We must insist upon speedier trials and upon punishments which are commensurate with the crimes." [2]

One approach that the NRA favors is mandatory sentencing for any crime committed with a gun. Another approach is to increase a criminal's sentence for such crimes. For example, a person convicted of armed robbery might be sentenced to five years for the robbery and an extra five years for having used a gun in the crime.

Gun control advocates agree with their opponents that more effective law enforcement would help solve the nation's crime problem. They support the concept of mandatory sentencing for crimes committed with a firearm. But they disagree with some of the NRA's other arguments.

They do not argue with the fact that people kill people. But they point about that, most often, they do so with handguns. The whole point of gun control laws, they say, is to make it more difficult for people to get handguns. When that happens, handgun deaths will decrease, they argue.

Some people have raised questions about the NRA's campaign for stiffer sentences. They point out that some states already have "add-on" laws that increase a criminal's sentence for using a gun in a crime. The problem is that pro- and anti-control groups do not agree about the effectiveness of stiffer laws, such as add-on sentencing. Gun control advocates say that research studies have failed to show that add-on sentencing effectively reduces the number of gun-related crimes. In response, the NRA points to dramatically reduced homicide rates in states such as Virginia, Arizona, Arkansas, and South Carolina that have stiff sentencing laws.[3]

Dealer Licensing

Probably the least restrictive form of gun control is dealer licensing. Licensing laws require that anyone who wants to sell firearms get a permit from the city, state, or federal government. In this way, authorities have some kind of check on people who sell guns. Mentally disturbed people and convicted criminals, for example, might be prevented from becoming gun dealers.

Dealer licensing only remotely affects the number of people who own guns. It might be that there would be fewer guns sold if there were fewer dealers. And the fewer dealers there are, the higher the price of guns is likely to be. But there seems to be no evidence that dealer licensing has any effect on the number of guns owned.

Gun Registration

Many gun laws require that a dealer keep careful records of the weapons he or she sells. Those records include information about both the weapon and the purchaser. One of the strongest arguments for gun registration is that it allows authorities to track guns that are used in crimes. Police can find out who bought the gun and where and when it was purchased. This information sometimes helps in solving a crime.

One problem with gun registration is that it may be required only once, when the gun is first sold. If a person later resells the gun, it may not have to be reregistered by the new owner. Hundreds of millions of guns are resold each year. Half of these guns are sold through dealers and half through individuals.[4] That means that police will have a difficult time tracing those guns if they are used in a crime.

Pro-control groups would prefer that all gun sales be registered the ways cars are. If you buy a used car, they point out, you have to reregister the car. Why could the same procedure not be used with firearms, they ask?

As with dealer licensing, gun registration is unlikely to have much effect on gun ownership. Someone who wants a gun to commit a crime might be discouraged from buying one by a registration law. The prospective criminal would know that the gun could be traced back to him or her. (But that possibility seems unlikely.) Many criminals just steal the guns they use in crimes. Again, there is no evidence that gun registration has much effect on the number of guns in circulation.

Permissive Licensing

The next most severe form of gun control involves licensing of the owner. Under licensing laws, a person who wants to buy a gun must first apply for a license to buy the gun. The purpose of the license is to prove that the prospective buyer is not a "high risk" or "prohibited" individual. Among those in these two categories are convicted criminals, mentally and emotionally unstable people, minors, and aliens.

In many cases, a licensing law includes a waiting period of seven, fourteen, twenty-one, or some other number of days. This waiting period allows officials to check on the applicant. They can find out if there is any reason to deny a license to the person. The waiting period also serves as a "cooling-off" time. Perhaps the prospective gun owner wanted to buy a weapon to commit a murder. During the waiting period, he or she might have second thoughts. The person might decide not to go ahead with the crime.

Some states now have waiting periods. During them, law enforcement officers often identify criminals trying to purchase a gun. In 1989, California authorities caught more than 2,000 felons trying to buy guns in this way. The state of Virginia also identified 109 criminals during the first two months that its new waiting-period law was in effect.[5]

The NRA disputes the interpretation of these numbers. It claims that some of the individuals denied permission to buy guns were *not* felons, but were the victims of faulty recordkeeping. As a result, some qualified, law-abiding citizens were prevented from owning guns by a licensing law.

One form of licensing is called permissive licensing. Laws of this kind require the police to grant a license to anyone who wants to buy a gun. Only people in "high risk" or "prohibited" groups can be denied a gun license. Anyone else must be given a license, no matter what his or her reason for wanting a gun may be. Furthermore, once the license is issued, that person may buy as many guns as he or she wants.

In 1988, for the first time, the U.S. Congress moved in the direction of background checks on prospective gun buyers. They ordered the attorney general to find an "immediate and accurate" method of screening people who want to buy guns. Gun dealers would have to be able to check a person while the person was still in the gun shop. The dealer would be able to find out if the prospective gun purchaser had a criminal record. If the person did, the gun dealer would not sell the person a gun.

At the time Congress passed its order, no one knew exactly how an instantaneous check could be done. One proposal had been to hook up the 15,000 gun dealers in the United States with FBI crime computers. Or a system of checking fingerprints automatically might be possible.

But either of these systems would be very expensive. They would also do little to catch the large number of eventual murderers, burglars, and rapists who have no previous criminal record. Also, by 1990, the attorney general disclosed that he could find no way of carrying out Congress's orders. FBI crime records were not well enough organized, he said, to allow any form of instantaneous checking. In fact, it seemed likely that such a system could not be put into place for many more years.[6]

Restrictive Licensing

Under restrictive licensing laws, authorities have the right to decide who can have a gun license and who cannot. A person who applies for a license must tell why he or she wants to buy a gun. Then officials (usually the police) decide if the reason is good enough to permit the granting of a license.

Police can use any criteria they want to make this decision. At one time, for example, police in New York City decided that target shooting was not a legitimate use of guns. Therefore, anyone who wanted a license to buy guns for target shooting was denied that license.[7]

Opponents of gun control see some serious problems with licensing laws. First, they claim that, if put into effect, licensing laws must specify a waiting period of *at least* thirty days. It takes at least that long, they say, to find out whether an applicant has a criminal record or should be denied a gun for some other reason. Legislating shorter waiting periods is a waste of time because the necessary information cannot be collected in a shorter period.

But waiting periods of this length are an imposition on both police and gun applicants. They mean that law enforcement officers will be spending their time in an office, checking records, rather than on the street, fighting crime. And innocent citizens will be presumed guilty by the law and will have to devote hours of their time obtaining a constitutionally guaranteed firearm.

Second, and more important, anti-control advocates believe that licensing laws are inherently unfair and nonsensical. When such laws are passed, law-abiding citizens will live by the rules. They will get licenses and, if required by law, even give up their guns. But criminals ignore the law anyway. So they will find a way to buy or steal handguns and keep them illegally. This concern leads to another popular NRA slogan. "When handguns are outlawed, only outlaws will have handguns."

Gun control advocates disagree with this argument. They say that, under any sensible form of gun control, responsible citizens will be able to own certain kinds of guns. What control laws will do, they argue, is to make it more difficult for people in high risk and prohibited groups to get weapons.

Finally, anti-control groups do not believe that waiting periods serve as "cooling-off" periods. They say that "crimes of passion" do not occur when otherwise peaceful individuals suddenly "go crazy" and commit a homicide. Instead, they point out, that 70–80 percent of *all* suspected murderers (along with 50 percent of their victims) have long criminal records.[8] The fact is, they say, the great majority of murderers will either choose another weapon or will simply wait until a gun becomes available for them to use. In either case, a waiting period would be of no value in preventing the crime.

Gun Bans

The most extreme form of gun control is a ban. Sometimes laws establish a partial ban. The "place and manner" laws described in Chapter 4 are examples of partial bans. People are allowed to own handguns, but they are allowed to have or use them only under certain circumstances. A common type of "place and manner" law is the prohibition against carrying guns in a car.

When people talk about banning guns, they usually refer to handguns only, not long guns. Some people would like to see a complete ban on all handgun ownership. The only exceptions to such a ban would be for police and other law enforcement officers. The

Morton Grove law discussed in Chapter 4 is an example of a complete ban on handguns.

Groups that advocate gun control sometimes disagree about a total ban on handguns. Some work for registration and licensing laws. They think that a total ban might go too far. Other groups think a total ban is necessary. That is the aim, for example, of the Coalition to Stop Gun Violence. That organization's position is:

> Both registration and licensing are useful but limited responses to the problem of handgun violence . . . Either of these proposals is a good first step, but only a partial response. Handguns would still be widely available, and people would still be killed—in accidents, in suicides, and in crimes of passion. As long as Americans still keep handguns under the mattress, in the closet, and in the glove compartment, none of us is safe.[9]

Anti-control groups often suspect that a total ban on all handguns is the real objective of all control groups. They believe that even those groups that are now working for licensing and registration laws plan eventually to push for a total ban on handguns.

This belief helps explain the NRA strategy on gun control. The battle is not just for a licensing law in Little Rock or a registration law in Juneau, anti-control groups believe. These laws are only steps on the road to complete prohibition of handguns. It is necessary, therefore, not to give in on *any* proposal that gun control groups make.

* * *

For anti-control groups like the NRA, proposals for new gun laws are almost always black-and-white issues. Although they do favor some types of place and manner laws, these groups are opposed to nearly all efforts to control gun use. Of course, pro-control groups often have a similar black-and-white view of these issues. In the next chapter, we will review some of the reasons that many people are totally opposed to any regulation of gun use.

7

Individual Rights: The Case Against Gun Control

A man walked into Robert Durham's Columbus, Ga., drugstore, drew a .22 revolver, and attempted to rob the owner. Durham drew out a gun of his own, and the two men shot it out. Two of Durham's shots struck the man. Police said the robber would be charged with armed robbery and aggravated assault. (*The Ledger & Enquirer,* Columbus, Ga., 10/12/86)[1]

* * *

A Stockton, Ca., woman awakened by a noise investigated and found a man coming through the back door of her home. She had armed herself with a pistol, and when the man made a sexual remark, she told him to leave or she would shoot. The would-be rapist fled. (*The Record,* Stockton, Calif., 10/16/86)

* * *

Entering his Muncie, Ind., home, Samuel Davis was knocked to the floor by an intruder. The man took Davis's wallet, but the seventy-six-year-old homeowner managed to get hold of his .32 revolver and fired. The burglar was found dead in a nearby vacant lot. (*The Star,* Muncie, Ind., 10/25/86)

* * *

Each month's issue of the National Rifle Association's *American Rifleman* magazine carries a column entitled "The Armed Citizen." The column reports ten to fifteen incidents like the ones above. They show how citizens have used firearms to protect their lives and property.

The citizen's constitutional right to own and use a gun legally, for whatever purposes he or she chooses, is at the core of the anti-control argument. You will recall from earlier chapters some of the arguments that have been offered *against* gun control. Some of those arguments include the following:

1. The majority of Americans do not really want new gun control laws.

2. Gun control laws already on the books do not work anyway.

3. Licensing and registration laws may sound like good ideas, but they are probably only the first step toward an outright ban on all or most guns.

You should also remember that anti-control groups are concerned about violent crime, too. They are not just *against* gun control laws. Instead, they want to do a better job of punishing people convicted of crimes with guns. They believe that violent crime can be reduced if stiff laws against gun-related crimes are passed and then enforced.

But those opposed to gun control also have some positive opinions about the use of guns. They have ideas as to why people should have the right to own and use guns. The two pillars on which their arguments rest are:

1. Guns provide people with an effective way of protecting themselves and their homes against crime.

2. The right to own guns, in any case, is guaranteed by the United States Constitution.

Guns for Self-Defense

Few people question the right of people to own guns for hunting, target practice, and law enforcement work. What people do debate is whether citizens should keep guns to protect themselves and their property. You read in Chapter 3 the reasons that gun control advocates think this practice is a dangerous one. But as the *American Rifleman's* "The Armed Citizen" column shows, many people do depend on guns for protection.

In an ideal world, of course, people would not have to worry about burglars, rapists, muggers, and other criminals. Since we do not live in an ideal world, we usually depend on law enforcement officers—the police—for protection. We hope that the presence of police officers will make a criminal hesitate to commit a crime or, if he or she does, that the criminal will be caught, convicted, and sent to prison.

The problem in modern American society, increasingly, is that people no longer believe they can count on the police for protection. For whatever reasons, the risk of being robbed or attacked is getting greater and greater. Dr. Mark Warr, a sociologist at the University of Texas, has said: "People have lost confidence in the ability of local government to control crime. There is a growing feeling that 'we must do it ourselves.' " [2] As a result, more and more citizens have decided to protect themselves with firearms.

The National Rifle Association emphasizes that this is a perfectly normal reaction by perfectly normal people. Those who buy guns for their own self-defense are not blood-thirsty criminals waiting to shoot a burglar. They are simply trying to protect themselves from criminals.

Barry Bruce-Briggs points out that many gun owners really think and care very little about the firearms they buy for protection. The guns, he thinks, are "mere tools" they may someday have to use in their own defense. In many cases, Bruce-Briggs believes: " . . . people have weapons tucked away with no explicit idea of how they might be used except 'you never know when you might need one.' No violent intent is implied, any more than a purchaser of life insurance intends to die that year. It is pure contingency."[3]

The Second Amendment

The second pillar of the gun owners' argument against gun control is that all Americans have the constitutional right to own guns. Whether you agree with the way people use them or not, at least they have the *right* to do so, goes the argument.

This issue is at the very heart of the gun control question. Does the United States Constitution grant to citizens the right to own guns? If it does, then laws that prohibit people from owning guns will be very difficult to pass and will probably be declared unconstitutional. If it does not, then legislators at all levels have the right to pass any gun laws they want to. In a sense, then, the constitutional question should really be resolved before any other gun control issue is discussed. The problem is that the constitutional question is a very difficult one about which there is a lot of disagreement.

The debate centers on the Second Amendment in the Bill of Rights of the Constitution. That amendment reads as follows: "A well-regulated militia, being necessary to the security of a free state, the right of the people to keep and bear arms shall not be infringed".

No one knows how many thousands of pages have been written by legal scholars trying to figure out exactly what that sentence means. Dozens of articles have been printed saying that the amendment does or does not allow private citizens in the United States to own firearms. The two possible interpretations of the amendment are:

1. Citizens have the right to "keep and bear arms" *only if and when* they are members of the militia. Private citizens who are not members of the militia have no constitutional right to own guns.

2. Citizens have the right to "keep and bear arms" whether or not they are members of the militia. In this view, ownership of guns by private citizens is a constitutionally protected right.

People disagree as to what the term "militia" means in the United States today. According to some authorities, the modern National Guard has taken the place of the "militia" mentioned in the Constitution. By this interpretation, the constitutional right to bear arms applies only to those men and women who belong to the guard. Others say that the term "militia" still applies to all able-bodied Americans. In this respect, the right to bear arms applies to everyone.

History of the Amendment

Most articles on the Second Amendment begin with a historical review. They argue that we can understand what the amendment means only if we understand what the writers of the Constitution were thinking about in their own day.

The debate about the right of citizens to own guns has been going on for hundreds of years. One of the first and most important contributions to it was the work of the political theorist, Niccolo Machiavelli, in the early 1500s.

Machiavelli warned that people could remain free only if they were willing and able to fight against an oppressive government. In order to do so, every citizen had to have the right to own a gun. If only the government had weapons, private citizens would have no way of defending their freedoms.

This idea was repeated and developed many times in the next two hundred years. English and French writers in the 1600s, for example, insisted that democracy could succeed only in those states where all citizens could be armed. These writers often warned also about the dangers of regular ("standing") armies. Who knows when a ruler might use those armies against his or her own people, they asked.

This tradition was well known to Jefferson, Adams, Madison, and other writers of the Constitution. No one really doubts that these men believed in the right of citizens to own guns. John Adams once wrote, for example, that "the people have a right to keep and to bear arms for the common defence."

That phrase—"a right to keep and to bear arms"—occurs over and over again in political writings, laws, and constitutions of the early colonies. Everyone agrees on that fact.

But what *exactly* did the phrase mean to the nation's forefathers? To some scholars, the phrase refers to a "communal" right. That is, people should have the right to own guns if and when they get together to fight for their own defense. In modern terms, they say, that means when they join the National Guard. Individual people do *not* have the right to own guns under any other circumstances as, for instance, if they want to defend their home against burglars.

This interpretation is similar to the way the Swiss deal with gun ownership. Individual citizens have the right—indeed, the legal obligation—to keep arms in their own homes. The purpose of having those arms is to be ready to fight for the nation's freedom as part of the Swiss militia. But that right and obligation does not mean that Swiss men also have the automatic right to own guns for their own personal use. Indeed, as we saw in Chapter 5, it is very difficult for an individual to get a gun for his or her own personal use in Switzerland.

According to a second interpretation of the Second Amendment, the right that is granted consists of two separate parts. The first part is the communal right to own guns as part of the militia, as described above. The second is a private right, that is, the right of each and every citizen to own his or her private weapon.

Those who argue for this interpretation believe that this view is clear from historical writings. They say that the right to bear arms may originally have referred only to those who belonged to the militia. But over time, they argue, the right took on a broader meaning until it eventually referred to a person's right to own any gun that he or she wanted to. As one writer has said: ". . . the armed citizen and the militia existed as distinct . . . elements within American thought, and it was perfectly reasonable to provide for both within the same amendment to the Constitution." [4]

Supreme Court Rulings

Disagreements as to what the Constitution "really" means are common. The ink was hardly dry on the original document before men and women started arguing about the intent of its writers. Fortunately, those writers provided a mechanism for resolving these disputes: the Supreme Court. One responsibility of the Court is to decide what the Constitution "really" means with respect to any one particular issue.

One way of interpreting the Second Amendment, then, is to see how the Supreme Court has ruled on this part of the Bill of Rights. You will hardly be surprised to learn that both pro- and anti-control groups think the Supreme Court has supported its own view of the amendment.

Advocates of the gun control say the answer is fairly clear. The Court has spoken about the Second Amendment on four occasions. The first three were in the nineteenth century (1876, 1886, and 1894) and the fourth in 1939. Supporters of gun control are convinced that, in each case, the Court ruled that private ownership of gun is *not* a constitutional right under the Second Amendment.

In addition, they believe that, by refusing to rule on other gun control cases, the Court appears to have confirmed this view. For example, the Court had an opportunity to consider a case brought against the 1981 Morton Grove gun control law. Lower courts had denied objections to that law. The Supreme Court refused to hear this case. In effect, it allowed lower court decisions to stand.

Opponents of gun control insist that these cases have little or nothing to do with the fundamental question as to whether citizens have the right to own guns. The first three cases, they say, actually deal with the issues of "incorporation," that is whether the Bill of Rights applies to the states as well as the federal government. What the Court ruled, they say, is that the Second Amendment does not apply to the states.

The fourth and most recent case, they say, dealt with a narrow issue involving one specific type of gun, the "sawed-off" shotgun. From their perspective, then, gun supporters claim: " . . . contrary to the widespread popular belief that the Supreme Court of the United States has definitively spoken on the issue of the constitutionality of gun control legislation, the issue remains far from settled." [5]

So we are back where we started, wondering exactly what the writers of the Second Amendment really meant to say. After many years of research and debate, the answer is still not clear. As with every other issue in the gun control controversy, people place very different interpretations on the same set of facts.

The NRA's efforts to get the Supreme Court to rule specifically on this matter, as described on page 67, have been unsuccessful. On January 15, 1991, the Court let stand a lower court's decision on the issue. The lower court had ruled that the Firearms Owners' Protection Act's ban on machine guns was constitutional.

Can You Trust the Government?

"When you lose your guns, you lose your freedom." [6]

Perhaps the debate over the Second Amendment sounds theoretical and academic, a subject for professors of law. But to many gun owners, it is very real. These people want to be able to have guns because they do not trust the government, not local government, not state government, and not the federal government.

In this respect, their attitudes are not much different from those of the early colonists. No one knows when the government will decide to come in and start taking away your freedoms, they say. It has happened over and over again in the past, and it could easily happen in the future.

Listen to what Mr. Gene Kurilow of the Stockton (Calif.) Rifle Club has to say on this point: "Freedom does not spring from government. Government's purpose is to resist and reduce freedoms. So I have very little confidence in my elected government, that they will preserve my rights. They're much more interested in preserving their imperatives." [7]

Mr. Kurilow was asked the following question: "At the beginning of the 1990s, you feel as an individual American that you can't trust your government?" Mr. Kurilow's response to that question was: "That is very true."

It is easy to understand how someone with this philosophy would oppose gun control. If you cannot trust government, then it certainly makes sense to want to own your own weapons. That will probably be your best—and perhaps only—way to protect your individual freedoms and liberty.

Too Many Guns to Control

Anti-control groups often raise a different kind of issue, the question of "reality," in talking about gun control. They remind us that 99.98 percent of all gun owners are law-abiding citizens. Of the 50–60 million handguns in the United States in 1986, fewer than 8,000 were used in murders. Two hundred times that number were used for hunting. Passing a law against handgun ownership means that the vast majority of handgun owners are labeled as criminals unless they turn in their handguns immediately.

Of course, since most gun owners are law-abiding citizens, one might hope and expect that they would turn in their guns in such a case. But what would the government do about those who did not? How could it possibly find and collect the millions of guns owned by private citizens? It would probably be hopeless even to try to register those 60 million handguns. The cost of hiring agents and paying for this kind of search and registration would be staggering. That kind of law might work in a small village, but it would never succeed in a large city, in a state, or across the United States.

An excellent example of this situation arose in California in 1990. The state legislature passed a law requiring owners of fifty-six models of semiautomatic "assault" weapons to register their weapons with local law enforcement authorities by January 1, 1991. When that deadline had arrived, about 15,000 applications for registration had been received. This number represented less than 5 percent of the estimated 200,000 to 300,000 semiautomatic weapons owned by Californians.

Reporters asked state officials what actions would be taken against the 95 percent of gun owners who had ignored the new law. Their answer was that enforcement of the law was a local responsibility. When asked how *they* would deal with the issue, local law officials replied that there was almost nothing they could do. They were far too busy with other responsibilities to locate and register owners of these guns.

Some writers have compared the effort to control handguns with the effort to control intoxicating beverages during the Prohibition years. Forget for a moment how you feel about the control of alcoholic beverages or the control of handguns. Remember what happened when the nation passed the Eighteenth Amendment to the Constitution, prohibiting the manufacture, sale, and use of intoxicating beverages. For thirteen years after the amendment was adopted, the nation was racked by crime, unrest, and violence. The country learned that it could not pass and enforce a law with which vast numbers of Americans disagreed. The full power of the U.S. government and all its law enforcement agencies could not change that fact. Efforts to control gun use on a national level, some people say, would be doomed to failure for the same reason.

Gun control advocates recognize this problem. They often suggest that gun control laws should apply only to new sales and new owners. People who already own guns might not have to give them up or to register them. The aim would be to keep guns out of the hands of criminals, not of law-abiding citizens.

How well this philosophy would work is not clear. Suppose we could pass a law next week that banned all *new* handguns or required their registration. Even then, there would be 60 million *old* handguns still available in the nation. Criminals would probably still have an easy time getting the guns they wanted for their crimes.

Gun Control and Snobbery

Some opponents of gun control see this debate in quite a different light. They think that many people on opposite sides of the argument are very different from one another.

Earlier we saw that gun owners are not very different from non-gun owners on most measures. But are those who write, speak, and lobby on gun control also essentially like each other? Or do they differ from each other in one or more important ways?

Some anti-control people believe that the answer to the last of these questions is "yes." They say that being in favor of gun control in the United States in the 1990s is the "politically correct" position. One writer, Dr. William R. Tonso, has tried to show that gun control groups are often led by professors, religious leaders, media stars, political cartoonists, syndicated columnists, and others who are in a position to influence the thinking of Americans.[8]

Dr. Tonso refers to these people as the "sages" of gun control. He claims that these sages often have a "missionary zeal" in their campaign for gun laws. They ignore research studies that oppose their positions, and they ridicule people who have different beliefs about gun laws. They may even think of anti-control people as less educated, less well to do, and less compassionate than members of their own gun control groups. Cartoonists, especially, tend to poke fun at the "paunchy beer drinkers" that they believe make up anti-control groups like the NRA.

A famous article on the gun control debate makes the same point. In "The Great American Gun War," Barry Bruce-Briggs calls this debate "a sort of low-grade war going on between two alternative views of what America is and ought to be." On one side of the war, he claims, are sophisticated citizens who believe in a just, rational, and civilized society in which "uncontrolled gun ownership is a blot upon civilization."

On the other side is a relatively small but highly committed group of people whose role model is the "independent frontiersman who takes care of himself and his family with no interference from the state." As far as these two groups are concerned, the gun control debate is not so far removed from the liberal/conservative political debate that is always going on in the United States.[9]

The point is that some people on both sides of the issue are passionate in their beliefs. Except for abortion and nuclear energy, few topics are likely to stir as much emotion among Americans today as does the gun issue.

The interesting point that anti-control groups make about this debate is that many of the gun control "sages" actually own their own handguns, despite their strong campaign for gun control. For example, the *New York Times* has a long record of supporting gun control legislation. Yet, Arthur Sulzberger, publisher of the *Times* has applied for a permit to carry his own concealed weapon. Also, the city of San Francisco under Mayor Diane Feinstein passed a ban on handguns. Yet, Mayor Feinstein herself had a permit to carry a gun.

Perhaps the best-known example of this situation involves columnist Carl Rowan who has written often and passionately about the need for stronger gun control. Yet he owns a handgun himself. Moreover, on the evening of June 14, 1988, Rowan shot and wounded an intruder in his backyard.

Opponents of gun control laws do not criticize Rowan for protecting his own property with a handgun. The right of every citizen to have a gun is exactly the right they have been arguing about. What they do object to is what they see as the hypocrisy of Rowan's writing about one position on gun control and acting from the opposite position.

Supporters of gun control say this criticism is unfair. A person can own firearms and still support some form of gun control. In fact, the 1990 *Time* magazine poll of gun owners showed that 87 percent favor a federal law requiring a seven-day waiting period and background check for anyone wanting to buy a handgun. Mandatory registration of semiautomatic weapons was favored by 73 percent of those polled, and rifle and shotgun registration by half of all respondents. Therefore, gun ownership and support for some forms of gun legislation are not mutually exclusive.

* * *

Will these disagreements ever be resolved? Is there a common ground on which pro- and anti-control groups can come together? In the next chapter, we will see what the future might hold for this great debate.

8

The Future of Gun Control in the United States

"Something is going to have to be done to lower the decibel level of this debate. There is more hyperbole, more exaggeration, more misquoted statistics, and more misplaced passion than we need for a subject this serious." [1]

The battle over gun control has been a long and bitter one. Both sides have fought hard, often for extreme positions. The National Rifle Association has consistently opposed nearly every restriction on gun ownership. The Coalition to Stop Gun Violence insists that only a complete ban on all handguns (except those used in law enforcement) is essential. Debates in the Congress and state legislatures have been long, drawn-out struggles, often decided one way or another by a handful of votes. Thus, it is difficult to predict what is likely to happen over the next five or ten years. Certainly compromise—the secret of most legislation—is likely to be difficult to obtain.

More Powerful Weapons

Yet a few trends in the war over gun control seem to be clear. First, the kinds of weapons available to the general public will probably continue to change. Not so many years ago, the debate centered on pistols and rifles. Today, the issue is more likely to be automatic and semiautomatic weapons, plastic guns, and armor-piercing bullets. Improved weapons technology has changed the tone and the stakes of the gun control debate in the last ten years, and it will probably continue to do so in the next ten.

Cases in which someone has used a military-style semiautomatic weapon in a mass murder have become more common. Or, at least, the general public seems more likely to have heard about and to be concerned about such cases. Tragedies such as these may well tip the balance for a private citizen or a legislator who has been uncertain about gun control. California's law controlling semiautomatic weapons, for example, almost certainly would not have passed as quickly and as easily as it did had not Patrick Edward Purdy killed and injured nearly three dozen schoolchildren with his AK-47 rifle.

In addition, the most up-to-date, most powerful weapons increasingly seem to find their way into the hands of drug dealers. As the nation's drug problem increases by leaps and bounds, so does the firepower of those involved with drugs. For law enforcement agencies, dealing with the drug problem has become an unfair, deadly battle in which the police are often outgunned by the criminals they are trying to catch.

In response to this problem, more police officers are buying semiautomatic weapons at their own expense. By late 1990, for example, a third of all San Francisco police officers had purchased their own semiautomatic pistol, most commonly the 9 mm Beretta 92F. As a matter of fact, a national pattern seems to be emerging. According to Gerald Arenberg, Director of the National Association of Chiefs of Police, about 80 percent of all police departments in the United States now require or allow the use of semiautomatic weapons by their officers.[2]

This situation has contributed to a change of heart about gun control among many police officers. Traditionally, law enforcement officers and the National Rifle Association have been natural allies. In recent years, however, some police officers have been more willing to consider at least some forms of gun control. Several law enforcement organizations have broken ranks with the NRA over legislation dealing with plastic guns, "cop-killer" bullets, and waiting periods for gun purchases. In each of these cases, the police organizations favored legislation that the NRA opposed.

For one of the nation's best-known police chiefs, Joseph McNamara of San Jose, California, the question is whether the NRA

The Beretta 92F, 9mm pistol. Many police officers are purchasing this semiautomatic weapon to help them compete with the more advanced firearms held by criminals.

"has gone off the deep end" and "lost any sense of responsibility." [3] Jerald Vaughn, director of the International Association of Chiefs of Police, seems to agree with Chief McNamara. He has described the NRA as "one of the most potentially dangerous organizations in the United States today." [4]

These sentiments are by no means unanimous among law enforcement officers. Many rank-and-file police officers say that organizations of police chiefs, police unions, and well-known spokepersons like Chief McNamara do not speak for them. Many are still willing and eager to work with the NRA against any form of gun control.

Changes Within the NRA

Another possible trend for the future may be a gradual change in the nation's leading anti-control lobby, the National Rifle Association. For more than twenty years, the NRA has been a powerful opponent of any gun control law. Part of its strength came from its ability to speak with one voice for three million members and 60–70 million gun owners.

In recent years, trouble has been brewing within the organization. From one part of the NRA have come complaints that the organization may be too rigid. The time may have come, some members say, for the NRA to consider at least some forms of gun control. The position of law enforcement officers like Chief McNamara represent this viewpoint.

Some ordinary members seem to share this viewpoint as well. For example, when interviewed for a national news magazine, one NRA member expressed support for background checks and mandatory training for gun buyers. "There has to be some limit on the Second Amendment," she said.[5]

Dissent within the NRA comes from another direction also, from those who think the organization has become too soft on gun control issues. A group of machine gun owners, for example, is angry because the NRA did not—or could not—prevent a ban on their favorite weapons in the 1986 Federal Firearms Owners Protection Act. They have formed their own group, the National Firearms Association to fight for reversing the machine gun prohibition.

Many NRA members still oppose *any* controls on gun ownership, the historic position for this organization. Some of these members have formed a group within the NRA, the Firearms Coalition, to fight for a stronger anti-control stand by the organization One leader of the Firearms Coalition believes that NRA lobbyists are too much involved in the "give-and-take" of Washington politics, and they seem to think that "it is always give." The organization's idea of negotiation, another coalition leader claims, "is deciding whether you should have your arm taken off at the shoulder or at the wrist." [6]

There is little doubt that the National Rifle Association will continue to be at the forefront of the fight against gun control in the future. How its battle plans will change—if at all—is, however, difficult to predict.

Gun Violence as a Medical Problem

"Injury from firearms is a public health problem whose toll is unacceptable. The time has come for us to address this problem in the manner in which we have addressed and dealt successfully with other threats to public health." [7]

The above view reflects the view of two public health experts at the U.S. Centers for Disease Control. The statement represents a growing concern among medical workers about the problem of injuries by firearms. That concern was also expressed by the American Medical Association's Council on Scientific Affairs. In 1989 the council said: "There is unquestionably a need to treat this public health matter [gun violence] with as much urgency as any dread disease." [8]

One reason for the growing concern of the medical profession is the problem of "assault weapon" injuries. Physicians are now using medical techniques for gunshot victims that were common in the Vietnam War. Traditionally, handguns produce relatively small, clean wounds. "Assault weapons," on the other hand, often result in "exploding organs and pulverized bones, [a] flood of internal bleeding." Dr. Stanley R. Klein, director of trauma services at Los Angeles Harbor Hospital, has said that "these are war injuries. Period. End of discussion." [9]

The economic cost of gunshot injuries has skyrocketed in the last few years. During 1987 and 1988, Highland Hospital in Oakland, California, treated about 700 gunshot victims at a total cost of $10.5 million. Most of these victims—2 percent of the hospital's patients—used 40 percent of its blood supply. By one estimate, the nationwide cost for treating gunshot victims has now reached $1 billion annually, with taxpayers covering 85 percent of that cost.

Some epidemiologists (an epidemiologist is a person who studies the causes, spread, and control of diseases in a community) have suggested thinking about gun violence as an epidemic. According to the president of the American College of Epidemiology: "Homicide is not a disease, but it is a public health condition whose primary cause is the possession of guns—and it could be considered an epidemic because of the high incidence in certain populations." [10]

The approach epidemiologists hope to take is to show how guns, death, and injury are related to each other. If they were studying a traditional disease, they would try to show that a certain organism *caused* a disease. Then they would trace how the disease moved through the community. Finally, they would suggest ways to prevent the spread of that disease.

In the case of guns, epidemiologists hope to show that gun ownership leads to violent crime. As Dr. P. O'Carroll at the Centers for Disease Control has said, "The way we're going to do this is to systematically build a case that owning firearms causes deaths." [11]

Opponents of gun control think this approach has no value. They claim that using medical terminology is just another way of attacking the right of citizens to own guns. Dr. Paul H. Blackman, research coordinator for the National Rifle Association, has this to say about a medical approach to gun control:

> Nonsense. Epidemics are things that are catching and gun ownership and use aren't catching . . . The CDC has been conducting and sponsoring incompetent research which includes lying about what data exist and what conclusions can be drawn . . . There's simply no justification for some of the garbage they've put out. [12]

In one respect, Dr. Blackman is correct. Calling gun violence by another name has not, thus far, produced any new data or any new suggestions for dealing with the problem. In fact, the AMA Council on Scientific Affairs' 1989 review of this issue reads like a summary of this book. It points out the conflicts in statistics and viewpoints on gun violence without offering any new insights on the problem.

Gun control opponents also question other medical arguments about gun injuries. They cite authorities who claim that wounds caused by military rifles are smaller, cleaner, and therefore presumably *less* serious, not more serious, than handgun wounds. They also disagree that gunshot injuries are a serious problem in medical economics since they account for no more than 0.2 percent of all medical costs in the United States.[13]

Alternative Approaches to Gun Control

Some advocates of gun control have become discouraged about the rate of legislative change. They see how difficult it is to get gun control laws passed at the local, state, and, especially, federal levels. Are there other ways, they ask, that gun control can be achieved?

One suggestion has been for the government to buy back guns from citizens. The idea is that the number of guns in circulation must be reduced. Too many guns are available for criminals to obtain. If citizens are willing to sell their guns back to the government, the rate of violent crimes may be reduced.

This approach has not been very popular with governmental bodies. But private groups have made the effort. For example, Father Marshall Gourley of Our Lady of Guadalupe Catholic Church, in Denver, Colorado, has been concerned about the number of shooting deaths in his parish. He decided to try a buy-back program in the community. Father Gourley offered $100 for each gun turned in to him.

Father Gourley's offer met with limited success. He received thirty-five handguns and four shotguns before his money ran out. It is not clear how effective the plan really was, however, One man who turned in his handgun said he planned to use the $100 reward as down payment on an assault rifle. Another gun owner threatened to kill the priest for his idea.

The arguments against buy-back programs are familiar ones. Criminals will certainly not sell their guns. That means that only law-abiding citizens will give up their weapons. Will they not then be even more vulnerable to burglars, rapists, and other armed criminals?

Also, buy-back programs are based on the belief that the amount of violent crime depends on the number of guns people own. As we have seen, there is some doubt as to whether that fact is actually true. Finally, even if buy-back programs did work in small communities, they would be far too expensive for large cities, states, or the federal government to adopt.

Legal Action Against Gun Manufacturers

A very different approach to gun control was first proposed in 1983: to sue companies that make firearms when someone is killed by one of their guns. In one of the first of these cases, the family of a Chicago police officer, killed while on duty, sued two companies, Walther and International Armament Corporation. Walther is the company that made the gun that killed the officer. International Armament is the U.S. distributor of that gun.

The suit was not a criminal case. The officer's family did not claim that the companies had done anything illegal in making and selling the gun. The suit, instead, was based on the concept of product liability. Product liability is a fairly new field of law. It was widely used for the first time in the United States in the 1970s in a suit against the Ford Motor Company for production of its Pinto model car.

A number of people were killed when the Pinto's gas tank exploded during accidents. Attorneys for those killed were able to prove that the car manufacturer knew that such fatal accidents were possible. They argued successfully that the company was guilty of selling a product that they knew could cause harm to purchasers.

Similar cases have been brought against the makers of other products that are potentially harmful to consumers. These cases form the basis of product liability cases against gun manufacturers and their distributors.

The argument is that gun manufacturers know that there is a reasonable possibility that their products will be used for criminal activity. The manufacturers of Saturday Night Specials, in particular, should be especially aware that virtually the only use for these weapons is in violent crime, at least to those who bring these suits. Therefore, these companies should be required to pay some of the costs of that violent crime.

Gun control advocates hope that winning such cases will frighten gun manufacturers and distributors. These companies will, they hope, begin to see the rising costs of making certain types of guns, such as Saturday Night Specials. They may decide that these costs are not worth the profit they make on those guns and may decide to stop making those weapons.

The Center to Prevent Handgun Violence, a nonprofit organization in Washington D.C., has become a clearinghouse for gun liability suits. The center's Legal Action Project maintains a list of lawyers who will handle such suits and a file on cases now pending before the courts. They also maintain a library of books and articles that lawyers can use in developing gun liability cases.

Product liability cases are unpopular with a wide range of people. It goes without saying that opponents of gun control think these cases are absurd. In addition, many lawyers doubt that gun liability is a legitimate form of product liability law. They say that such cases are simply a way of getting around the fact that governments have not passed effective gun control laws.

Even people who support gun control have their doubts about this approach to the issue. One specialist in product liability law, for example, has said that "though I believe in gun control, I think it should be accomplished by other means." [14]

Gun Education

People on both sides of the gun control issue do agree on one point. Young people need to know more about firearms. What and how they should be taught, however, is the source of some debate. The NRA and many gun owners believe that "gun education" means teaching boys and girls how to use firearms safely. In fact, classes in proper gun use have traditionally been an important part of NRA activities.

Gun control advocates place a different emphasis in gun education. They try to show young people that firearms can be very dangerous and should not be handled. A video program developed by the Dade County (Florida) school system, for example, shows boys and girls who have been seriously injured and killed by firearms. The message appears to be that guns are "bad" and "dangerous" and should be avoided.

* * *

Buy-back programs and gun liability cases may not be the solution to the nation's gun control debate. Perhaps the most that can be said for these approaches is that they represent new ways of looking at the issue. All sides of the debate agree that violent crime is a serious national problem for the United States in the 1990s. But they agree on little else.

Efforts to reduce violent crime by passing new gun legislation have not been very successful because the laws have not been enforced, too few have been passed, they are too weak, or for some other reason. The time may now have arrived when other new and innovative ideas for reducing violent crime need to be developed and tried out. Improved education about what guns are like, what they can do, and how they should and should not be used may, in the long run, be our best hope for solving this difficult national issue.

A Note on Sources

Wherever possible, I have tried to use the most recent statistics available from unbiased sources. Two of the most important of those sources are the FBI's annual *Uniform Crime Reports* and the Public Health Service's *Vital Statistics of the United States*. The text also contains statistics provided by special interest groups such as the National Rifle Association and Handgun Control, Inc.

These groups often question the validity of data from other sources, including those provided by governmental agencies. In addition, the very nature of statistical data makes controversy possible. For example, Handgun Control, Inc., claims that gun accidents were the fifth leading cause of death among children in 1988. The National Rifle Association says they were the sixth leading cause. Depending on the way causes of death are categorized and the way "children" is defined, either claim can be correct . . . or both can be considered incorrect.

I have tried, in all cases to report the number or range of numbers on any particular statistic that appears to be most defensible. Readers should understand, however, that many of the figures reported in this text are still the subject of dispute by one or another special interest organization.

David E. Newton

Notes by Chapter

Chapter 1

1. *Crime in the United States (Uniform Crime Reports)* 1989, United States Department of Justice, Federal Bureau of Investigation, (Washington, D.C.: 1990), p. 10.

2. *Vital Statistics of the United States*, United States Department of Health and Human Services, Public Health Service, Centers for Disease Control, National Center for Health Statistics. (Washington, D.C.: 1990), pp. 246, 302–303.

3. Ibid., p. 11.

4. As estimated in "Save Children's Lives With Curbs on Guns," editorial in *USA Today*, (October 31, 1989), p. 10A.

5. *Vital Statistics*, pp. 302–303.

6. Donald Baer, Ted Gest, and Lynn Anderson Carle, "Guns," *US News & World Report*, (May 8, 1989), p. 26.

7. "NRA Fact Sheet," n.d.

8. "Handgun Control," pamphlet published by Handgun Control, Inc.

9. "Handgun Facts: Twelve Questions and Answers About Handgun Control," pamphlet published by Handgun Control, Inc.

10. "Don't Buy HCI Lies," pamphlet published by the National Rifle Association.

11. Baer, Gest, and Carle, "Guns," p. 11.

12. Baer, Gest, and Carle, "Guns," p. 22, and Dr. Paul H. Blackman, NRA, personal communication.

Chapter 2

1. Martin Killias, "Gun Ownership and Violent Crime: The Swiss Experience in International Perspective," *Security Journal*, Vol. 1, (1990), p. 171.

2. Don B. Kates, Jr., ed., *Firearms and Violence: Issues of Public Policy* (Cambridge, Mass.: Ballinger Publishing Company, 1984), p. 406.

3. Robert E. Shalhope, "The Ideological Origins of the Second Amendment," *The Journal of American History*, (December 1982), pp. 599–614.

4. Donald Baer, Ted Gest, and Lynn Anderson Carle, "Guns," *US News & World Report*, (May 8, 1989), p. 22.

5. Kates, *Firearms and Violence: Issues of Public Policy*, p. 492.

6. Ibid., p. 494.

7. Franklin E. Zimring and Gordon Hawkins, *The Citizen's Guide to Gun Control* (New York: Macmillan Publishing Company, 1987), p. 186.

8. Ibid., p. 187.

9. Letty Cottin Pogrebin, "Pistols of the Women of America," *Nation*, (May 15, 1989), p. 649.

10. Kirk Johnson, "Gun Valley Tries to Adapt to the Winds of Change," *New York Times*, (March 21, 1989), p. 31.

11. Zimring and Hawkins, *The Citizen's Guide to Gun Control*, p. 188.

12. The data on which the graphs on pages 28–29 are based are now more than two decades old. More recent surveys have been conducted, but none has been as comprehensive as the one reported here. These later surveys do suggest that gun ownership patterns have not changed markedly since the 1969 study. Also see James D. Wright, Peter H. Rossi, and Kathleen Daly, *Under the Gun: Weapons, Crime, and Violence in America* (New York: Aldine Publishing Company,

1983), pp. 105–106, and Robert E. Markush and Alfred A. Bartolucci, "Firearms and Suicide in the United States," *American Journal of Public Health*, (February 1984), p. 125.

13. Zimring and Hawkins, *The Citizen's Guide to Gun Control*, p. 188.

14. Katherine Jamieson and Timothy J. Flanagan, *Sourcebook of Criminal Justice Statistics* (Washington, D.C.: U.S. Department of Justice Bureau of Justice Statistics, 1988).

15. Ibid.

16. Zimring and Hawkins, *The Citizen's Guide to Gun Control*, pp. 188–189.

17. Ibid., p. 82.

18. Kirk Johnson, "Gun Valley Tries to Adapt to the Winds of Change," *New York Times*, (March 21, 1989), p. 32.

19. William Cormier, "Bulletproof Fashions for School Kids," *San Francisco Chronicle*, (September 9, 1990), p. A6.

20. ABC News Special, "Guns," January 25, 1990.

21. Wright, Rossi, and Daly, *Under the Gun: Weapons, Crime, and Violence in America*, Chapter 6.

Chapter 3

1. Quoted in Coalition to Stop Gun Violence 1990 Calendar, April.

2. *Crime in the United States (Uniform Crime Reports)*, United States Department of Justice, Federal Bureau of Investigation, (Washington, D.C.: 1988), p. 21.

3. "20 Questions and Answers," pamphlet published by the Coalition to Stop Gun Violence.

4. Marsha F. Goldsmith, "Epidemiologists Aim at New Target: Health Risk of Handgun Proliferation," *Journal of the American Medical Association*, (February 3, 1989), p. 676.

5. Lonn Johnston, "15 Homicides in Oakland Ring in Bloody New Year," *San Francisco Chronicle*, (January 26, 1990), p. A9.

6. James D. Wright, Peter H. Rossi, and Kathleen Daly, *Under the Gun: Weapons, Crime, and Violence in America* (New York: Aldine Publishing Company, 1983), Chapter 9.

7. *Special Report: Handgun Crime Victims*, U.S. Department of Justice, Bureau of Justice Statistics, (Washington, D.C.: 1990), p. 1.

8. As quoted in Ellen Goodman, "Danger is Close to Home," *San Francisco Chronicle*, (January 9, 1990), p. A17.

9. Don B. Kates, Jr., ed., *Firearms and Violence: Issues of Public Policy* (Cambridge, Mass.: Ballinger Publishing Company, 1984), Chapter 8.

10. Claud Hamilton, "Pack a Trail Gun," *Gun World*, (December 1979), pp. 38–41.

11. Dr. Paul H. Blackman, NRA, personal communication.

12. "20 Questions and Answers."

13. Stockton (Calif.) Police Department Pathologist in ABC News Special, "Guns," January 25, 1990.

14. James D. Wright and Peter H. Rossi, *Armed and Considered Dangerous: A Survey of Felons and Their Firearms* (New York: Aldine de Gruyter, 1986), p. 211.

15. Kates, *Firearms and Violence: Issues of Public Policy*, p. 26.

16. Wright and Rossi, *Armed and Considered Dangerous: A Survey of Felons and Their Firearms*, Table 11.2, p. 216.

17. Ibid, Table 11.3, p. 221.

18. Kates, *Firearms and Violence: Issues of Public Policy*, p. 535.

19. "20 Questions and Answers."

20. See also James D. Wright, "In the Heat of the Moment," *Reason*, (August/September 1990), pp. 44–45.

21. "Seven Deadly Days," *Time*, (July 17, 1989), p. 30.

22. *Vital Statistics of the United States*, United States Department of Health and Human Services, Public Health Service, Centers for Disease Control, National Center for Health Statistics. (Washington, D.C.: 1990), p. 300.

23. *Vital Statistics*, p. 300. See also Kates, *Firearms and Violence: Issues of Public Policy*, p. 536.

24. Wright, Rossi, and Daly, *Under the Gun: Weapons, Crime, and Violence in America*, p. 168.

25. *Vital Statistics*, p. 302.

26. Wright, Rossi, and Daly, *Under the Gun: Weapons, Crime, and Violence in America*, p. 167.

27. Data summarized from *Vital Statistics of the United States*, 1960 and 1980, as reported in Zimring, Franklin E., and Gordon Hawkins, *The Citizen's Guide to Gun Control* (New York: Macmillan Publishing Company, 1987), Tables 6-1–6-3, pp. 61–62.

28. "Facts About Teen Suicide and Handguns," published by Handgun Control, Inc.

29. Position statement from the Coalition to Stop Gun Violence.

Chapter 4

1. Franklin E. Zimring, and Gordon Hawkins, *The Citizen's Guide to Gun Control* (New York: Macmillan Publishing Company, 1987), p. 122.

2. Don B. Kates, Jr., ed., *Firearms and Violence: Issues of Public Policy* (Cambridge, Mass.: Ballinger Publishing Company, 1984), p. 477.

3. Zimring and Hawkins, *The Citizen's Guide To Gun Control*, p. 126.

4. Barry Bruce-Briggs, "The Great American Gun War," *The Public Interest,* (Fall 1976), p. 42.

5. Ibid, p. 44.

6. Bruce-Briggs "The Great American Gun War," p. 44.

7. William E. Schmidt, "Pressure For Gun Control Rises and Falls, but Ardor for Arms Seems Constant," *New York Times,* (October 25, 1987), p. E5

8. Donald Baer, Ted Gest, and Lynn Anderson Carle, "Guns," *US News and World Report,* (May 8, 1989), p. 21.

Chapter 5

1. "Under the Gun," *New Republic,* (August 26, 1987), pp. 7–8.

2. "Handgun control," pamphlet published by Handgun Control, Inc.

3. "Don't Buy HCI Lies," pamphlet published by the National Rifle Association.

4. As quoted in Michael Isikoff, "NRA Asks High Court to Lift Ban on Private Machine Guns," *San Francisco Chronicle,* (December 29, 1990), p. A8.

5. James D. Wright, Peter H. Rossi, and Kathleen Daly, *Under the Gun: Weapons, Crime, and Violence in America* (New York: Aldine Publishing Company, 1983), p. 259.

6. Edward D. Jones, III, "The District of Columbia's 'Firearms Control Regulations Act of 1975': The Toughest Handgun Control Law in the United States—Or Is It?," *Annals of the American Academy of Political And Social Sciences,* (May 1981), pp. 138–149.

7. Wright, Rossi, and Daly, *Under the Gun: Weapons, Crime, and Violence in America,* p. 296.

8. "Crime Rates Rise in New York City," *New York Times,* (September 17, 1988), p. A1.

9. Sam Roberts, "Gun Possession: Lighter Penalty Than Advertised," *New York Times*, (June 22, 1987), p. B1.

10. "Handgun Facts: Twelve Questions and Answers about Handgun Control," pamphlet published by Handgun Control, Inc.

11. "Ten Myths About 'Gun Control,'" pamphlet published by the National Rifle Association.

12. John H. Sloan, et al., "Handgun Regulations, Crime, Assaults, and Homicide: A Tale of Two Cities," *New England Journal of Medicine*, (November 10, 1988) pp. 1256–1262.

13. Paul H. Blackman, "Handgun Regulations, Crime, Assaults, and Homicide: A Tale of Two Cities," *New England Journal of Medicine*, (May 4, 1989), pp. 1214–1215.

14. NRA Firearms Fact Card 1990.

15. Barry Bruce-Briggs, "The Great American Gun War," *The Public Interest*, (Fall 1976), p. 56.

16. "Handgun Control," pamphlet published by Handgun Control, Inc.

17. "Ten Myths about 'Gun Control.'"

18. "Handgun Control."

19. "Ten Myths about 'Gun Control,'"

20. Bruce-Briggs, "The Great American Gun War," p. 56.

21. "20 Questions and Answers," pamphlet published by the Coalition to Stop Gun Violence.

22. Jonathan Beaty, Michael Riley, and Richard Woodbury, "Under Fire," *Time*, (January 29, 1990), pp. 16–21.

23. Wright, Rossi, and Daly, *Under the Gun: Weapons, Crime, and Violence in America*, p. 240.

24. "Ten Myths about 'Gun Control.'"

Chapter 6

1. Dale Thurston, Citizens for a Better Stockton, on ABC News Special "Guns," January 25, 1990.

2. "Ten Myths about 'Gun Control,' " pamphlet published by the National Rifle Association.

3. "Criminals Don't Wait; Why Should You?," pamphlet published by the National Rifle Association.

4. Franklin E. Zimring, and Gordon Hawkins, *The Citizen's Guide to Gun Control* (New York: Macmillan Publishing Company, 1987), p. 116.

5. ABC News Special, "Guns," January 25, 1990.

6. Ted Gest, "The Next Wave of Gun Control," *US News & World Report*, (February 27, 1989), p. 30.

7. Don B. Kates, Jr., ed., *Firearms and Violence: Issues of Public Policy* (Cambridge, Mass.: Ballinger Publishing Company, 1984), p. 140.

8. "Criminals Don't Wait; Why Should You?"

9. "20 Questions and Answers," pamphlet published by the Coalition to Stop Gun Violence.

Chapter 7

1. These anecdotes are taken from the *American Rifleman*'s "The Armed Citizen" column for January 1987, p. 6.

2. Jonathan Beaty, Elaine Shannon, and Richard Woodbury, "The Other Arms Race," *Time*, (February 6, 1989), p. 24.

3. Barry Bruce-Briggs, "The Great American Gun War," *The Public Interest*, (Fall 1976), p. 40.

4. Robert E. Shalhope, "The Second Amendment and the Right to Bear Arms: An Exchange," *The Journal of American History*, (December 1984), p. 593.

5. *The Right to Keep and Bear Arms* . . . (Washington, D.C.: National Rifle Association Institute for Legislative Action, 1989), p. 15.

6. Dale Thurston, Citizens for a Better Stockton, on the ABC News Special, "Guns," January 25, 1990.

7. ABC News Special, "Guns," January 25, 1990.

8. Don B. Kates Jr., ed., *Firearms and Violence: Issues of Public Policy*, (Cambridge, Mass.: Ballinger Publishing Company, 1984), Chapter 4.

9. Bruce-Briggs "The Great American Gun War," pp. 61–62.

Chapter 8

1. Jonathan Beaty on the ABC News Special, "Guns," January 25, 1990.

2. L. A. Chung, "S. F. Police Buying Semiautomatic Guns," *San Francisco Chronicle*, (August 15, 1990), p. A2.

3. George Hackett, "Battle Over the Plastic Guns," *Newsweek*, (June 1, 1987), p. 31

4. Ted Gest, "Dissidents, Old Allies Shake NRA," *US News & World Report*, (April 27, 1987), p. 44.

5. Donald Baer, Ted Gest and Lynn Anderson Carle, "Guns," *U.S. News & World Report*, (May 8, 1989), p. 25.

6. Gest, "Dissidents, Old Allies Shake NRA," p. 44.

7. James A. Mercy, and Vernon N. Houk, "Firearm Injuries: A Call for Science," *New England Journal of Medicine*, (November 10, 1988), p. 1284.

8. American Medical Association Council on Scientific Affairs, "Firearms, Injuries and Deaths: A Critical Public Health Issue," *Public Health Reports*, (March-April 1989), pp. 111–120.

9. Jane Gross, "Epidemic in Urban Hospitals: Wounds From Assault Rifles," *New York Times,* (February 21, 1989), p. 1.

10. Marsha F. Goldsmith, "Epidemiologists Aim at New Target: Health Risk of Handgun Proliferation," *Journal of the American Medical Association,* (February 3, 1989), p. 675.

11. Goldsmith, "Epidemiologists Aim at New Target: Health Risk of Handgun Proliferation," p. 676.

12. Ibid.

13. Paul H. Blackman, NRA, personal communication.

14. Elaine F. Weiss, "Guns in the Courts," *Atlantic,* (May 1983), p. 14.

Further Reading

Baer, Donald, Ted Gest, and Lynn Anderson Carle. "Guns." *US News & World Report,* May 8, 1989, pp. 20–25.

Blackman, Paul H. "Armed Citizens and Crime Control." *American Rifleman,* July 1988, pp. 48–49.

——— "The Armed Criminal in America." *American Rifleman,* August 1985, pp. 34 *ff.*

Bruce-Briggs, Barry. "The Great American Gun War." *The Public Interest,* Fall 1976, pp. 37–62.

Church, G. J. "The Other Arms Race." *Time,* February 6, 1989, pp. 20–26.

"The Facts About 'Plastic Guns.'" *American Rifleman,* September 1987, p. 42.

"The Federal Gun Control Act of 1963." *Congressional Digest,* May 1986, pp. 130–159.

Goldsmith, Marsha F. "Epidemiologists Aim at New Target: Health Risk of Handgun Proliferation." *Journal of the American Medical Association,* February 3, 1989, pp. 675–676.

Jamieson, Katherine, and Timothy J. Flanagan. *Sourcebook of Criminal Justice Statistics.* Washington, D.C.: Government Printing Office, 1988.

Kates, Don B., Jr., ed. *Firearms and Violence: Issues of Public Policy.* Cambridge, Mass.: Ballinger Publishing Company, 1984.

Kruschke, Earl R. *The Right to Keep and Bear Arms: A Continuing American Dilemma,* Springfield, Ill.: Charles C. Thomas, 1985.

Lacayo, Richard. "Under Fire." *Time,* January 29, 1990, pp. 16–21.

Siegel, Mark A., Nancy R. Jacobs, and Carol R. Foster. *Gun Control: Restricting Rights or Protecting People.* Wylie, Tex.: Information Plus, 1989.

United States Department of Justice, Bureau of Justice Statistics. *Report to the Nation on Crime and Justice.* Washington, D.C.: Government Printing Office, 1988.

United States Department of Justice, Federal Bureau of Investigation. *Crime in the United States (Uniform Crime Reports).* Washington, D.C.: Government Printing Office, 1988.

Wright, James D., and Peter H. Rossi. *Armed and Considered Dangerous: A Survey of Felons and Their Firearms.* New York: Aldine de Gruyter, 1986.

Wright, James D., Peter H. Rossi, and Kathleen Daly. *Under the Gun: Weapons, Crime, and Violence in America.* New York: Aldine Publishing Company, 1983.

Zimring, Franklin E., and Gordon Hawkins. *The Citizen's Guide to Gun Control.* New York: Macmillan Publishing Company, 1987.

For Further Information

Bureau of Alcohol, Tobacco and Firearms
Department of the Treasury
Washington, D.C. 20226
(202) 566-7591
Important publication: "(Your Guide to) Federal Firearms Regulation, 1988-89."

Center to Prevent Handgun Violence
1225 Eye Street, N.W., #1100
Washington, D.C. 20005
(202) 289-7319
Important publications: "Handgun Safety Guidelines"; "Guns & the Constitution."

Coalition to Stop Gun Violence
100 Maryland Avenue, N.E.
Washington, D.C. 20002
(202) 544-7190
Important publications: "The Banner" (newsletter); "20 Questions and Answers"; annual calendar.

Handgun Control, Inc.
1400 K Street, N.W.
Washington, D.C. 20005
(202) 898-0792
Important publications: "Handgun Control"; "Washington Report" (quarterly newsletter); "Assault Weapon Questions & Answers." Parent organization of the Center to Prevent Handgun Violence.

National Rifle Association
1600 Rhode Island Avenue, N.W.
Washington, D.C. 20036
(202) 828-6000
Important publications: *American Rifleman* (monthly magazine); *Insights* (monthly magazine for younger members); "Gun Law Failures"; "A Question of Self-Defense"; "Criminals Don't Wait; Why Should You?"; "Semi-Auto Firearms: The Citizen's Choice"; "The Right to Keep and Bear Arms . . . An Analysis of the Second Amendment"; "The Myth of the 'Saturday Night Special.'"

Index

A accidents, gun-related, 46–48
African Americans and gun ownership, 28–30
"assault" weapons, 8
bans on, 58, 94
Autry, Gene, 22

B Bartley-Fox Amendment (Massachusetts state law), 54, 71–72
Beretta 92F, 99–100
Billy the Kid, 22
Borinsky, Dr. Mark, 13
Brady, Sarah, 13, 65
Brady bill, 15, 65–66
Bureau of Alcohol, Tobacco and Firearms (BATF), 61
Butler, Frank, 22

C California gun laws, 54–55, 94
Center to Prevent Handgun Violence (CPHV), 15
Charles II, of England, 18
Charter Arms, 27, 32
Coalition to Stop Gun Violence (CSGV), 11–15
Cody, Buffalo Bill, 21
cooling-off periods, 83
"cop-killer" bullets, 66

D Dade County (Florida) gun law, 54
dealer licensing. *See* licensing, of gun dealers

District of Columbia gun law, 68–69
domestic violence and guns, 45–46
drugs and guns, 37–39

E Earp, Wyatt, 22
England (gun laws), 73–74
Evans, Dale, 22

F Federal Firearms Act of 1938, 62
Federal Firearms Owners Protection Act of 1986, 64
Feinstein, Diane, 96
Firearms Coalition, 102

G gangs and guns, 37–39
Gibson, Hoot, 22
Gourley, Father Marshall, 105
gun accidents, 46–49
gun buy-back programs, 104–105
Gun Control Act of 1968, 11, 62–63
gun control methods, 77–84
gun education, 107
gun laws, 50–76
effectiveness, 67–74
public opinion about, 74–76
state, 53–54
trends, 54–55
types, 51–52

gun ownership
and crime, 39–42
patterns, 26–30
reasons, 22–25, 87–88
gun violence
as a medical problem, 102–104
examples, 5–6
statistics, 7
guns
and crime, 35–39
and domestic violence, 45–46
bans on, 83–84
frontier use, 19
in American culture, 21–22
registration of, 79–80
theft of, 37
types, 8

H Handgun Control, Inc. (HCI), 11–15
handguns, 8
uses in crime, 39–40
Hawkins, Gordon, 27
Hickok, Wild Bill, 22

I *Insights* magazine, 31

J James II, of England, 18
Japan (gun laws), 73

K Kennedy-Rodino bill of 1984, 63–64
Kennesaw (Ga.) gun law, 55–56

L "Lady Smith" revolver, 26
legal action against gun companies, 105–107
licensing
of gun dealers, 79
of gun owners
permissive, 80–82
restrictive, 82–83
long guns, 8

M Maryland (gun laws), 55, 76
Massachusetts Bay Colony gun law, 50
Masterson, Bat, 22
McClure-Volkmer bill of 1984, 64
McNamara, Joseph, 100
Mix, Tom, 22
Morton Grove (Ill.) gun law, 55–56

N National Coalition to Ban Handguns, 11
National Council to Control Handguns, 11
National Firearms Act of 1934, 62
National Rifle Association (NRA), 11–12, 31, 66–67, 101–102
New York City gun law, 69–70

O Oakland (Calif.) gun violence, 38
Oakley, Annie, 22, 23

P "place and manner" gun laws, 51
plastic guns, 66
Purdy, Patrick Edward, 57

R "restricted ownership" gun laws, 51
Richmond (Calif.) gun violence, 38
Rogers, Roy, 22
Rowan, Carl, 96

S Sadowski, Dr. Laura, 31
"Saturday Night Specials" (SNS), 41–43

Seattle (Wash.). *See* Sloan, John H., study
semiautomatic weapons, 8, 56–60
Second Amendment (U.S. Constitution), 19, 88–93
Shields, N.T. "Pete," 13
Sloan, John H., study, 72
Smith & Wesson Company, 26–27
"snobbery" and gun control, 95–97
Stockton (Calif.) mass murder, 57–58
substitution theory, 43–45
suicides, gun-related, 48–49
Sullivan Law (New York State), 53–54
Sulzberger, Arthur, 96

Supreme Court rulings on guns, 91–93
Switzerland (gun laws), 72–73

T trail guns, 42–43

V Vancouver, (B.C.). *See* Sloan, John H., study
Vermont state gun law, 56
Virginia Colony gun law, 50

W War Revenue Act of 1919, 61
Washington, D.C., gun law. *See* District of Columbia gun law
Wayne, John, 22
women and guns, 26–27

Y youth and guns, 30–33

Z Zimring, Franklin E., 27

About the Author

David E. Newton is a widely published author of over forty books for young people. He was a teacher of high school math and science for over fifteen years and was also a Professor of Chemistry at Salem State College in Massachusetts. Mr. Newton is currently an Adjunct Professor at the University of San Francisco, teaching courses on science and social issues.